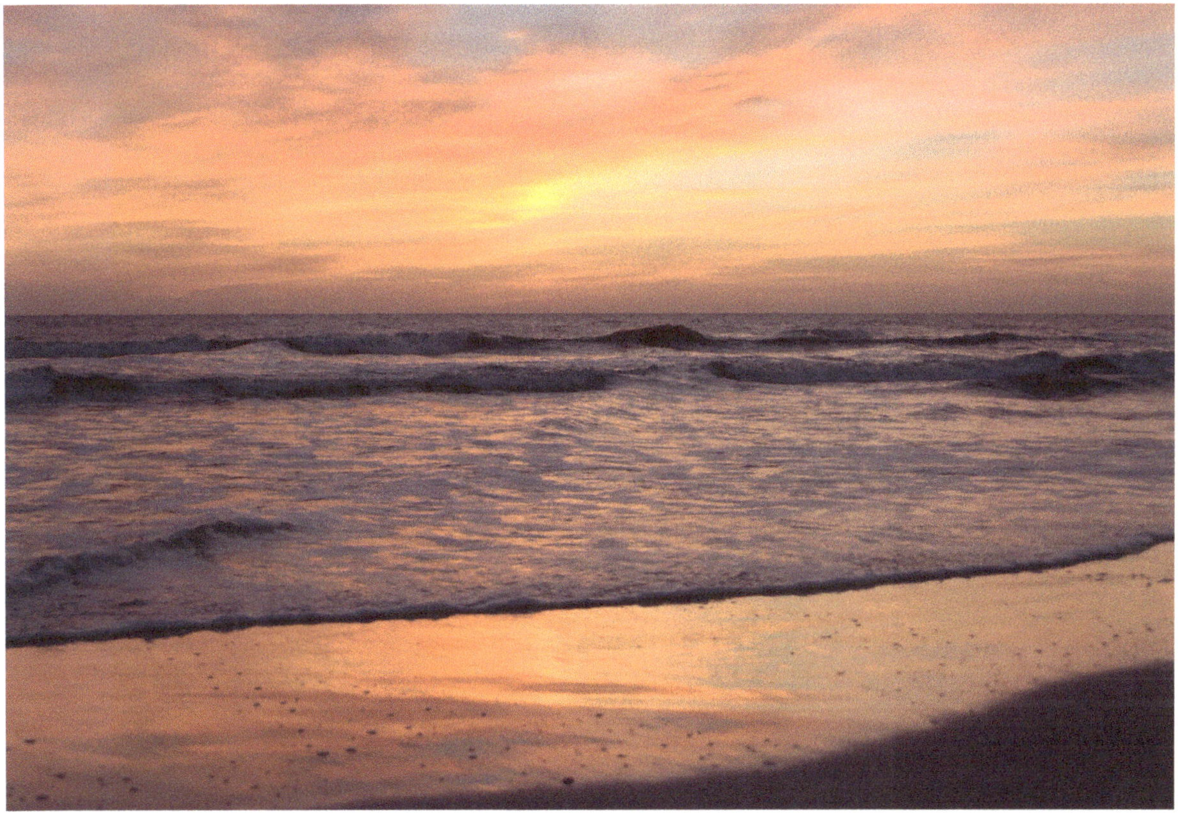

Anastasia Island
St. Augustine's Jewel by the Sea

Kenneth M. Barrett, Jr.

Contents

Introduction

Introduction

Anastasia. Saint Anastasia. Santa Anastasia. Island of Anastasia.

Each sounds as musical and mysterious today as it must have a few hundred years ago when it was finally named Anastasia Island.

Just east of today's Bridge of Lions across the Matanzas Bay from downtown St. Augustine, Florida, Anastasia Island has shared and contributed to the rich history of the United States' oldest town.

Domain of pirates, privateers, treasure hunters and beachcombers, the allure of Anastasia has attracted the curious and the determined throughout its long storied history.

The Early Years

In 1565, a lonely watchtower was built somewhere on the northern limits of a yet unnamed island east of the new little town of St. Augustine. This allowed a Spanish sentry to gaze out across the sand bars of the inlet in search of sailing vessels making their way along the coastline. How isolated and forlorn those sentries must have felt, peering out on the wild Atlantic Ocean hundreds of miles from other settlements.

In 1566, the new and struggling settlement made its way across the bay and found a home on the barrier island. There is some speculation about exactly where the early settlers tried to make a home on those shifting sands and beneath the maritime forest that covered the island. Nevertheless, they succeeded and remained on the island until moving back across the bay in 1572 where St. Augustine is located today.

By the time the English had settled in South Carolina and Georgia, the island was called Anastasia. Like a sister to her brother, St. Augustine, Anastasia is a jewel by the sea.

Today's Anastasia Island

The 14 miles-long barrier island has changed some since colonial times – most recently by the huge crowds of residents and visitors swarming over her shores. Yet one can still find a measure of solitude and quiet on her beaches and in her waters.

Brilliant sunrises, long lasting sunsets, constantly changing patterns of light and color attract artists and fishermen, writers and photographers, beachcombers and dreamers.

Mother Nature's sweeping brush portrays its many secrets of a landscape teeming with shore and wading birds, and thousands of terns nesting and resting along the fore dunes.

These scenes and many more, including historical sites, attractions and parks, are vividly displayed in color photographs that are sure to delight visitors and residents.

Anastasia Island
St. Augustine's Jewel by the Sea

Davis Shores

Construction of Davis Shores on the north end of Anastasia Island forever changed the composition of the island and helped usher it into the 20th Century.

Davis Shores was named after D. P. Davis, a resident of Green Cove Springs, Florida, who had built Davis Island in Tampa Bay.

In 1924, Davis brought his extensive collection of dredges and scores of workers to St. Augustine and transformed a low tidal zone into what he hoped would be his latest development. He planned to name it after himself. This was the largest new development in the island's history.

A seawall was built completely around the north end of the island. Then the oyster beds and salt marshes were filled with dredged material from Matanzas Bay and the St. Augustine Inlet. This was pumped into and onto the north end of the island to create his neighborhood. Streets were laid out, scores of palm trees were planted, a few homes began to be constructed by 1927 when the Bridge of Lions opened, and his office downtown was ready for business.

The Depression, hurricanes and poor economics stilled much of his dream. The Florida land boom was over. Speculators and dreamers lost a fortune. Davis took an ocean cruise to get away from his troubles for a while and disappeared at sea, never to be seen again. Most of the houses and trees that make up this area are products of post-World War II development. Sidewalks and landscaping turned the sandy neighborhoods into a busy residential area. A historic marker at the foot of the Bridge of Lions explains this history.

In 2015, a new pair of lions were installed in the little park east of the Bridge of Lions. These were a gift to the city by new residents who fell in love with the island and wanted to make their own mark on Anastasia.

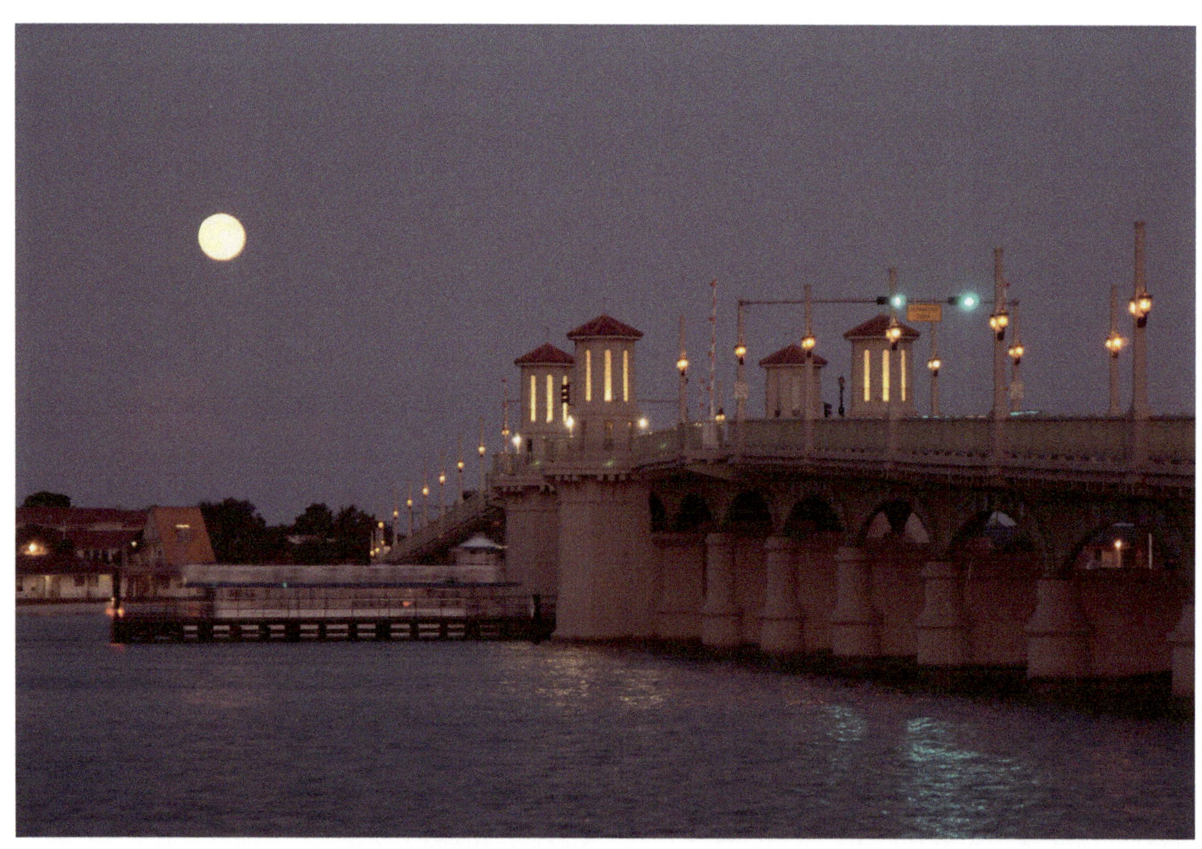

The recently restored Bridge of Lions connects Davis Shores and
Anastasia Island with downtown St. Augustine.

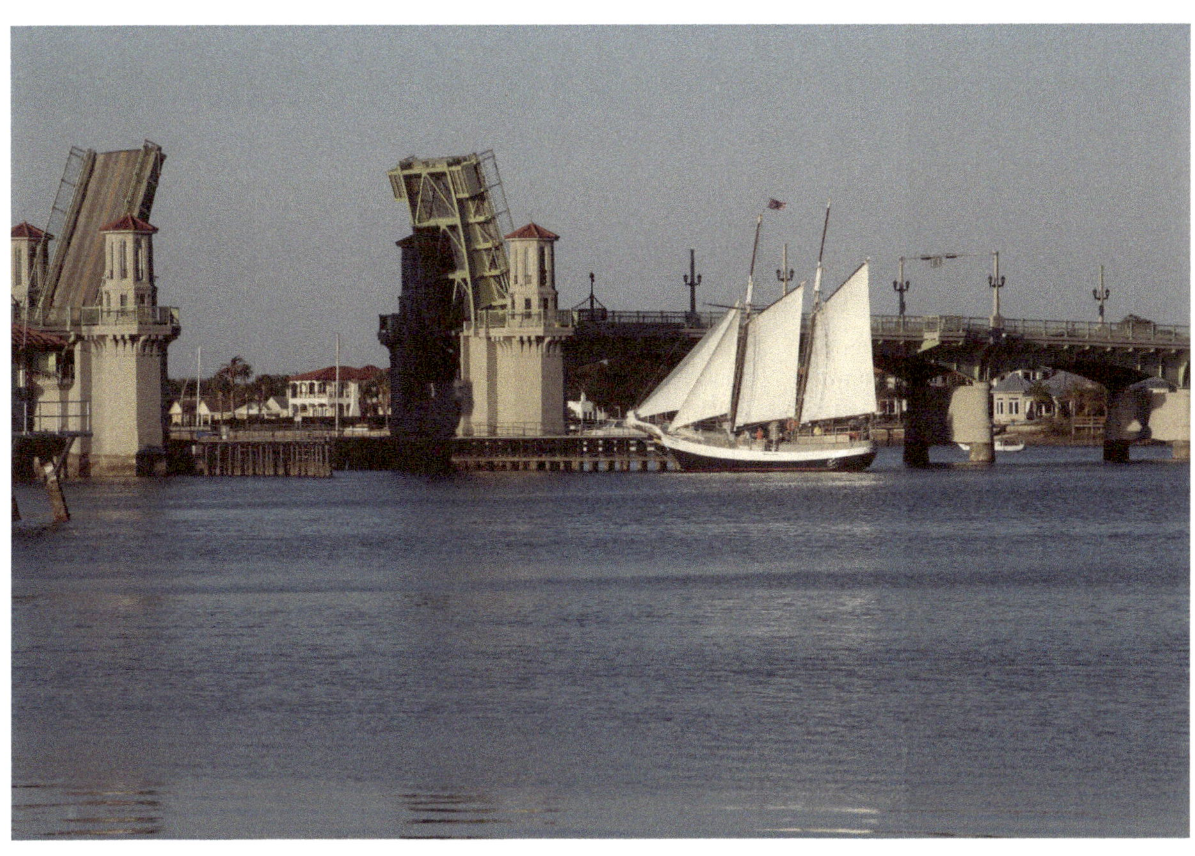

Reflecting St. Augustine's maritime heritage, the Schooner Freedom
sails through the bridge out into the St. Augustine Inlet.

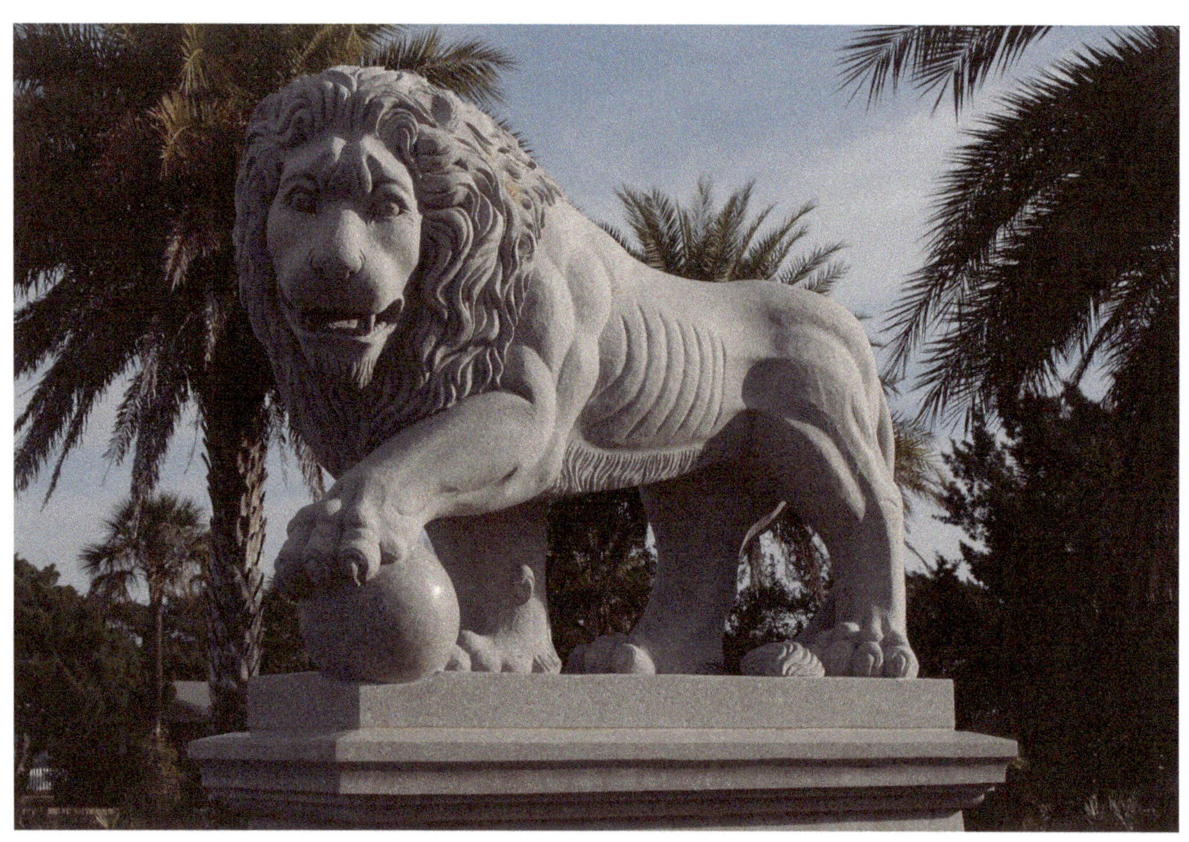

One of the two new lions gifted to the city.

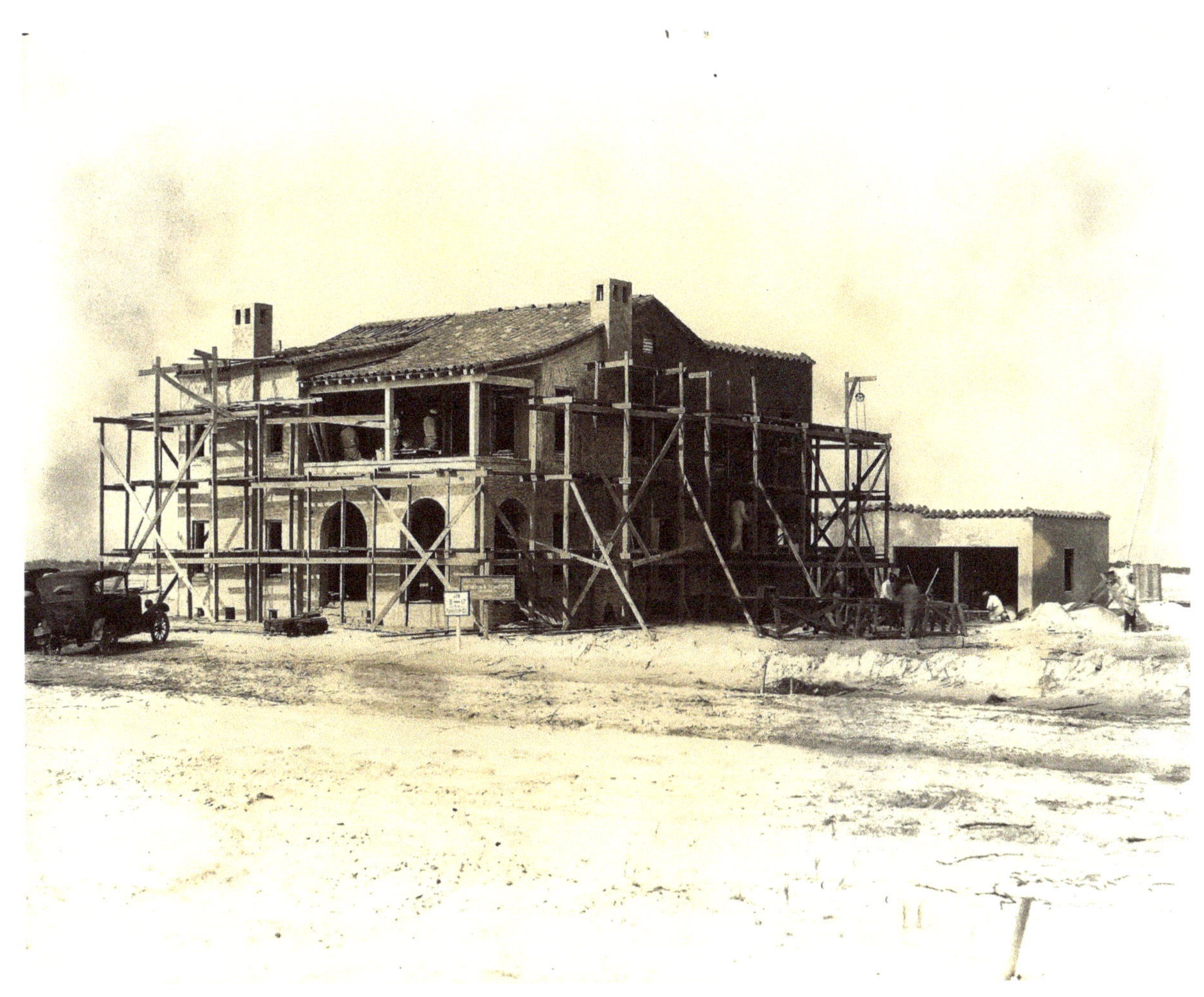

Construction of one of the first houses in Davis Shores, circa 1926.
Photo by Burgert Bros, Tampa. From Kenneth M. Barrett, Jr.'s collection.

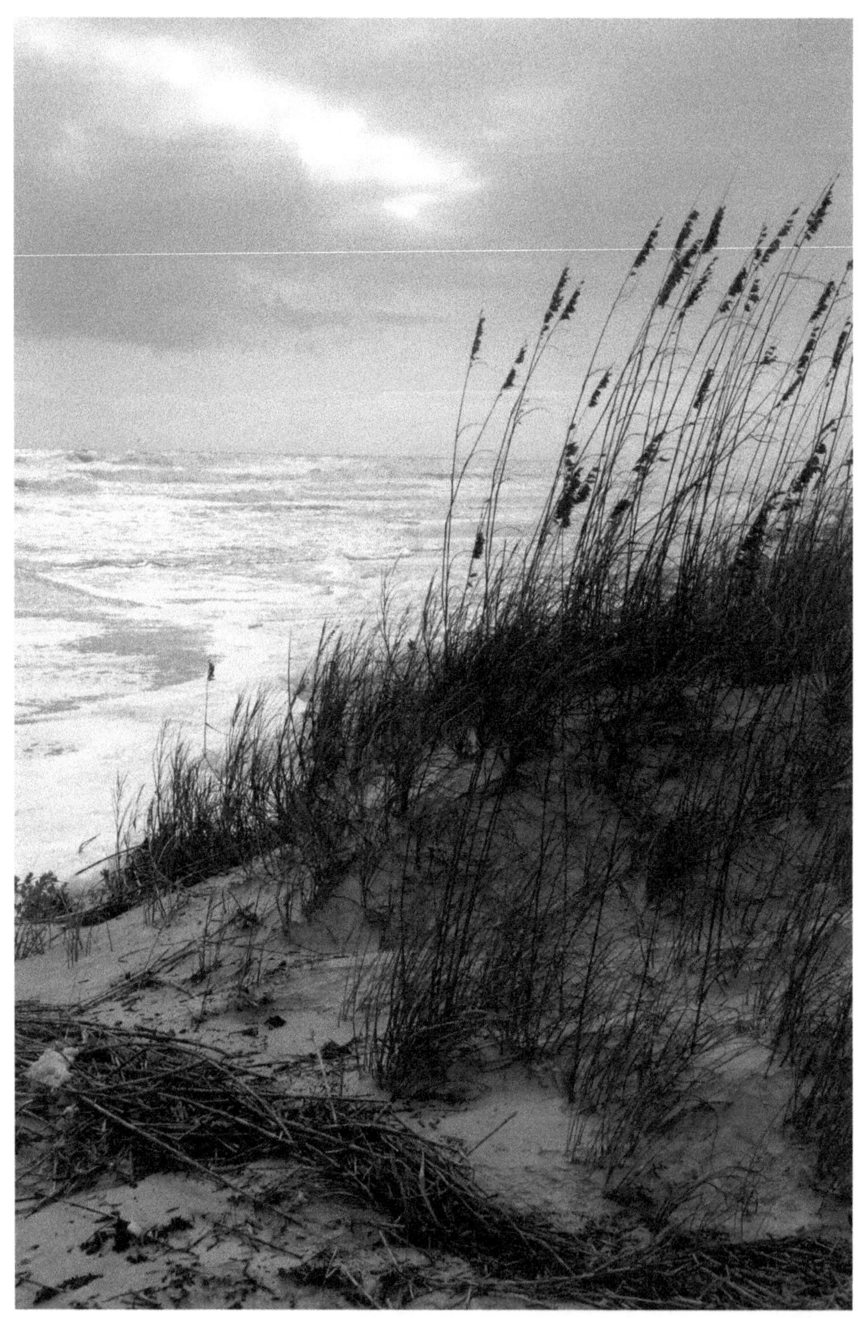

High tide during a nor'easter.

Oglethorpe Battery Park

Oglethorpe Battery Park is a small grassy corner located on Oglethorpe Boulevard, an avenue running east from the foot of the Bridge of Lions. The sounds of kids playing baseball and riding bicycles fill the air.

The park is named after General James Edward Oglethorpe, who laid siege to the city in the summer of 1740 by constructing a cannon battery close to this spot and firing on the walls of the Castillo de San Marcos for twenty-seven days.

British warships bottlenecked the entrance to the inlet east of Anastasia. Over 900 soldiers and Indians surrounded the town and attacked the northern defensive position of Fort Mose. Spanish blockade runners from Havana brought in needed supplies. General Oglethorpe was not successful in taking the fort or the town. He eventually went back to Georgia.

Today a coquina marker and three small cannons mark the spot where England tried to take the capital of Florida from the Spanish. The coquina marker was dedicated in 1930 by the St. Augustine Historical Society. The cannons were dedicated in 2015 as part of St. Augustine's 450th birthday celebration. If the size of the reproduced cannons is any indication of the cannons used by the founder of Georgia to bombard the Castillo, one can see why they had little effect on the stone walls.

The city of St. Augustine maintains this tranquil spot.

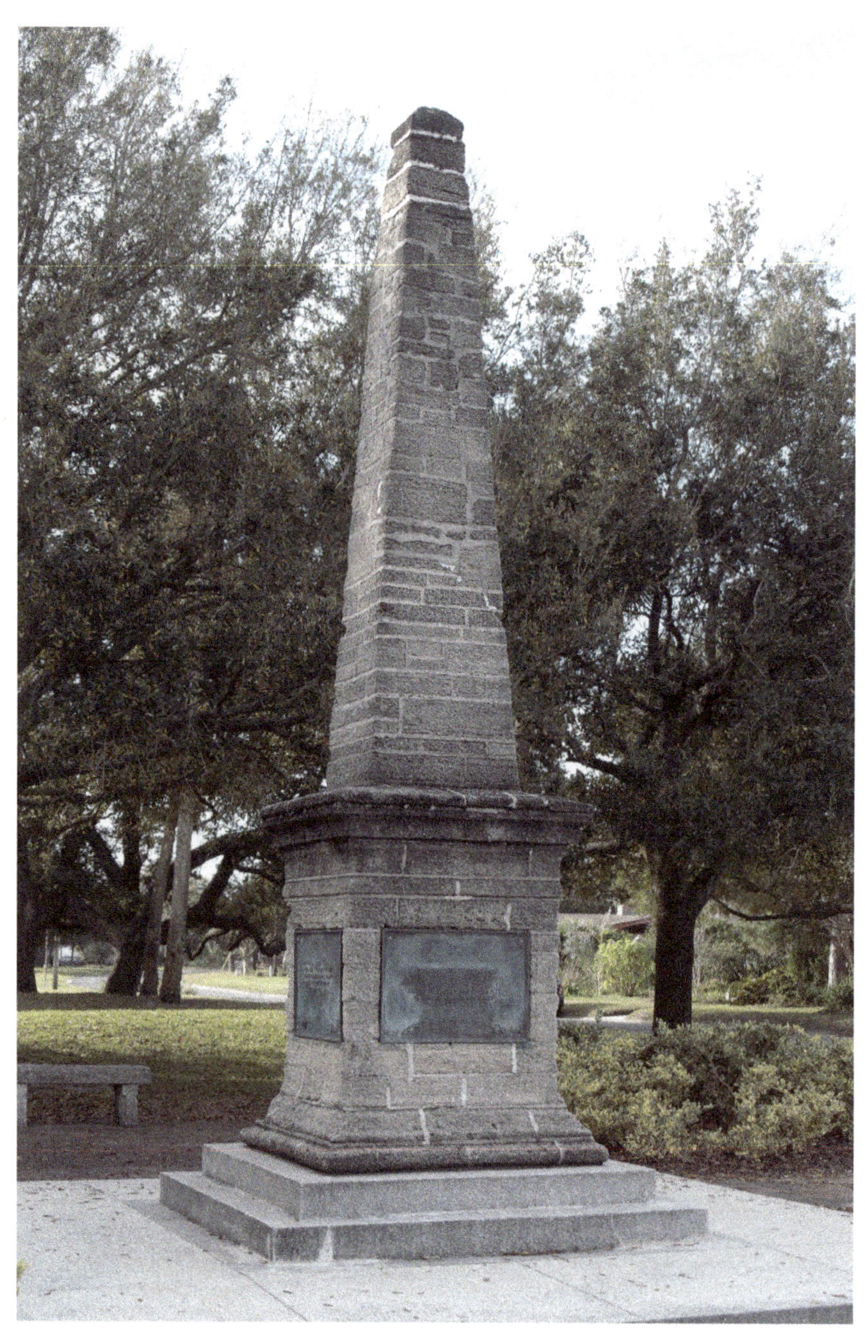

Oglethorpe Monument

Lighthouse Park

From the earliest days of Spanish settlement there has been some type of watchtower or lighthouse standing watch over the northeast corner of Anastasia Island. As early as 1565 Spanish soldiers had built a wooden watchtower overlooking the entrance to the St. Augustine Inlet. Historian Susan Parker reminds us that just nine months after its founding, St. Augustine was moved to the island to protect the settlers from Indians or buccaneers. By 1572, the little town moved back across the bay.

In 1586, cruising north along the Florida shoreline, a lookout in one of Francis Drake's sailing vessels spied a watchtower on the north end of the island. Sailing in for a closer look, one of the gentleman soldiers described the tower as being four masts of sixty feet in height with a platform for looking out over the ocean.

Drake's fleet numbered over 25 vessels and was comprised of over 2,000 sailors and soldiers. Overwhelmed by the sheer number of attackers the Spanish made an attempt at defending their town but fled into the woods. Drake had already taken Cartagena and made off with a considerable amount of treasure and other valuables, so his raid on St. Augustine made little sense. He did find and take the Spanish treasury worth over 2000 pesos that had been left behind when the settlers fled into the woods. Burning the town, destroying the fruit trees and gardens, Drake and his fleet sailed on.

By the late 1600s, a coquina watchtower and quarters had been constructed on the northeast corner of the island. When England took over Florida in 1763, it added a sixty-foot wooden tower to the existing stone tower built by the Spanish. A small cannon was fired when shipping was sighted off the bar. Still, the St. Augustine Inlet continued to shift and shoal and claimed its fair share of ships.

After 1821 when Florida became a territory of the United States, improvements were made to the watchtower and its existing quarters. In 1824, the United States government replaced the old tower with a new coquina lighthouse. Lighthouse park, slowly, was being settled by the military and the towns people. During the Civil War, Confederate volunteers led by the mayor of

St. Augustine removed the lens and other equipment from the lighthouse so it could not be used for navigation. Within a year, the old light was operational.

Lighthouse Park grew up around the old tower. A few small cottages and houses went up. Construction of the current lighthouse brought additional newcomers. By the late 1880s, the beach along the eastern shore had become a destination for some and home for others. The Octagon House built in 1886 at 62 Lighthouse Avenue is one of the more unusual buildings. A few shop owners, fishermen and nature lovers made the shaded area their home. After the turn of the century and into the 1940s, there was a grocery store and filling station in the neighborhood. St. Augustine artist Earl Cunningham made his home in Lighthouse Park.

Today, the neighbors complain a bit about the tourists and the traffic that the Lighthouse Museum attracts, but no one wants to move from this sleepy and historic area. There is a fishing pier, boat ramp and picnic tables underneath the oak and cedar trees. Tennis courts have been recently refinished.

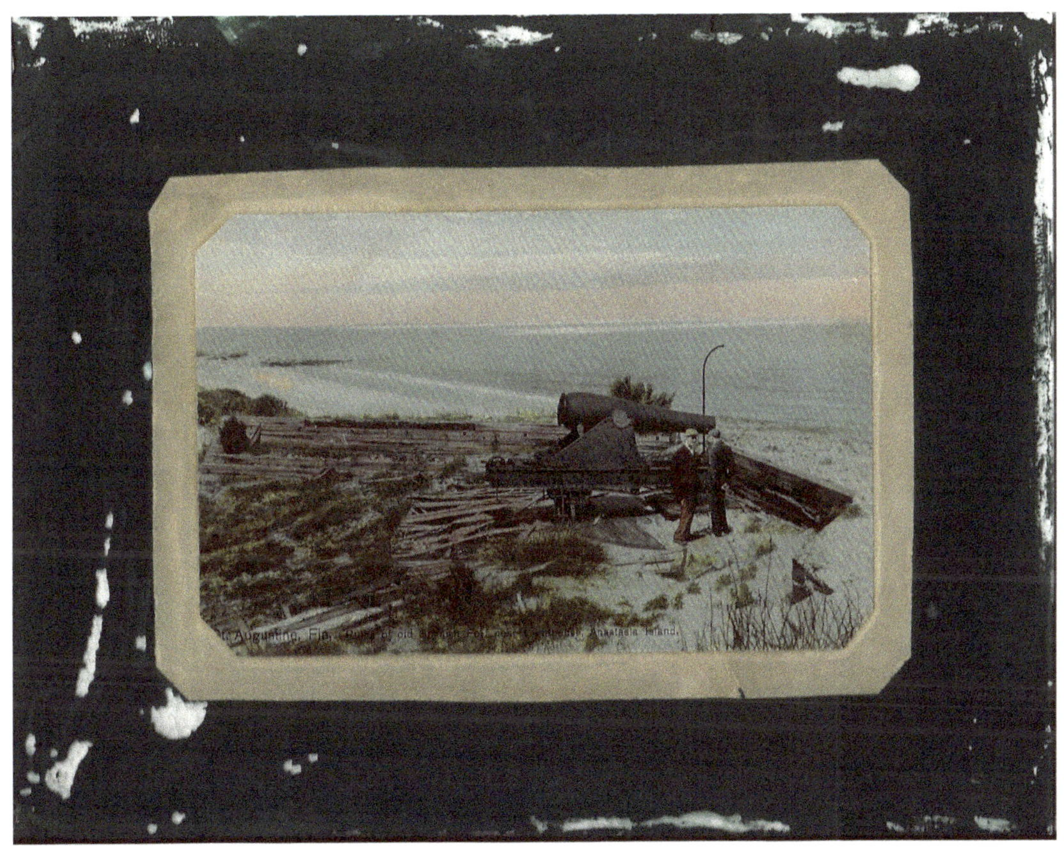

Lighthouse cannon, a 32-pound cast iron cannon battery mounted near the lighthouse in 1898. Originally installed at the Castillo de San Marcos National Monument in the 1840s, this cannon tube may be on exhibit in the downtown Plaza. Photo from Kenneth M. Barrett, Jr.'s collection.

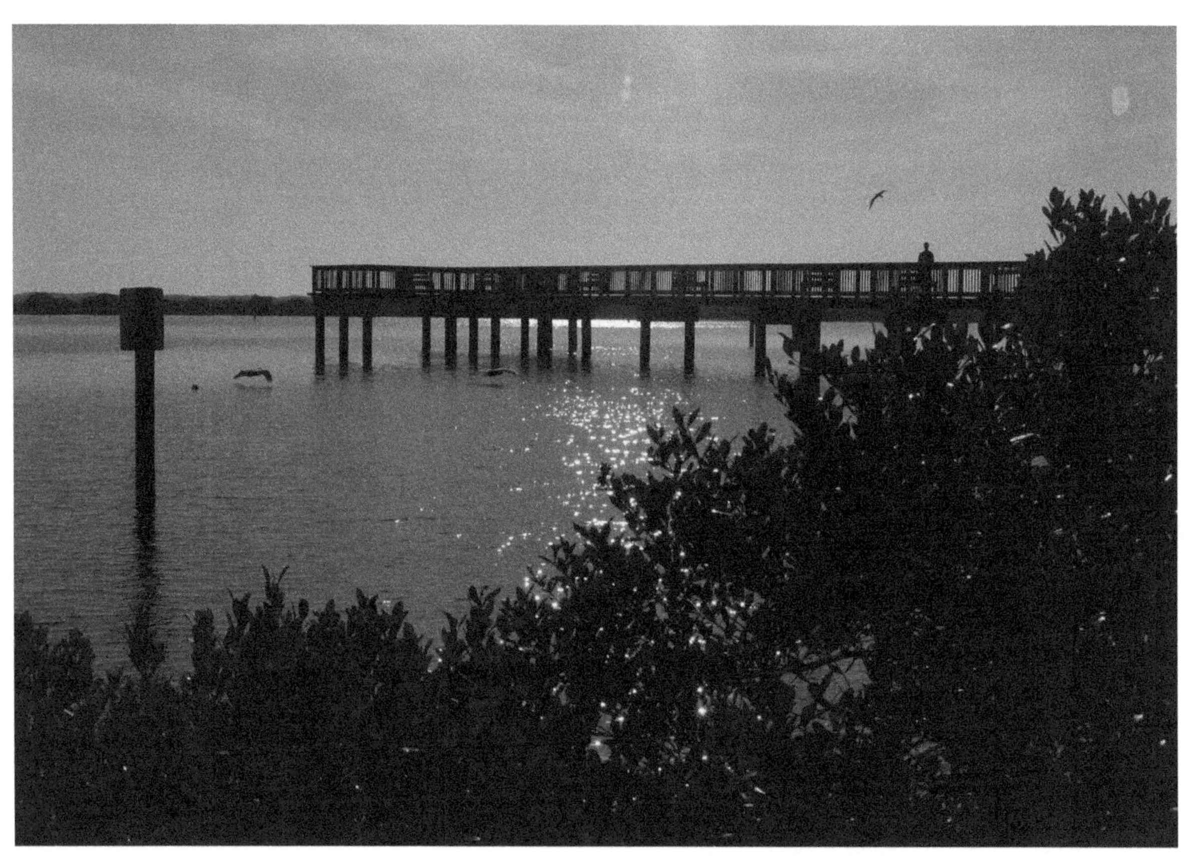

Lighthouse Park fishing pier and boat ramp.

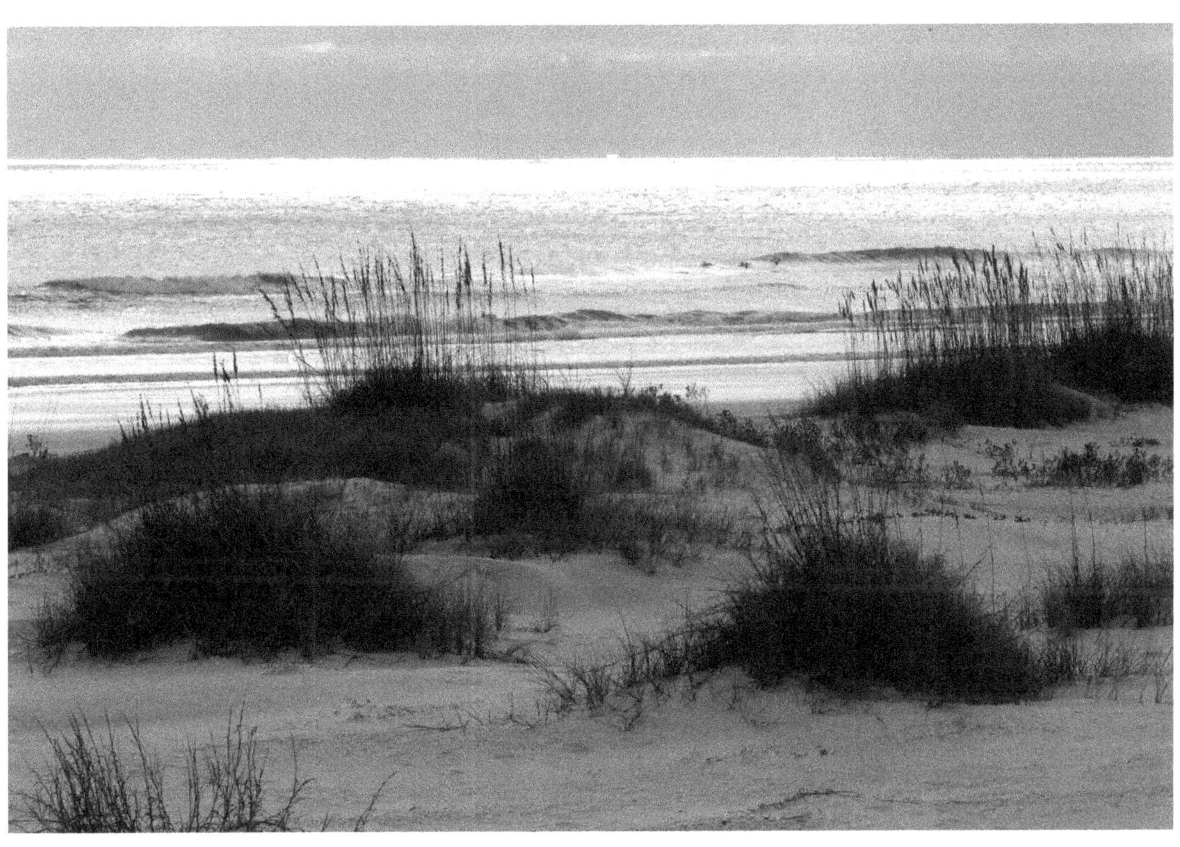

The area east of the lighthouse is known as Conch Island.
Salt Run flows south from the inlet into Anastasia State Park.

St. Augustine Lighthouse and Museum

From earliest times native Timucuan Indians lived and fished along these shores. Early Spanish settlers chose the high ground for a few years to escape attack. A watchtower looked out over the sandbars and shoals of the St. Augustine Inlet as early as late 1565.

Begun in 1871, and finished in 1874, the St. Augustine Lighthouse is the oldest brick building in St. Augustine. The keepers house was finished in 1876 and now serves as a museum. Without a doubt it is the most visited attraction on Anastasia Island.

Built west of the old coquina tower constructed in 1824, the current lighthouse sits on the high point of the big coquina crown that makes up the island. The Atlantic Ocean was slowly washing away the northeast corner of the island and it was only a matter of time before waves and water would over wash the old site.

Designed by Paul Pelz, who drew up the plans for the Library of Congress, the brick tower was considered a lighthouse of the first order. Standing 165 feet high, mounted with the original Fresnel lens, the light could be seen 15 miles to sea. When first built, it faced the original inlet, but Mother Nature and man eventually forced the dredging of the present day inlet.

The familiar black and white barber pole stripes, crowned with the red tower top, have made the St. Augustine Lighthouse a favorite for photographers. Within a few years of completion, visitors to St. Augustine wanted to explore the tower and its neighborhood. A small horse drawn railroad carried the curious over the sand from the original wooden bridge to Lighthouse Park. People began to build cottages and beach homes around the area.

The 1824 tower and quarters were slowly washing away. After the new lighthouse was completed, one of the light keepers noted in the daily log that in September 1875 "continuing high tides and wind are washing away ends of this barrier island and large quantities of bank."
On September 10, 1878, a "storm washed away the foundation from under the dwelling of the old lighthouse and the building tumbled over into the river." A note in the Lighthouse Keeper's log reminds us that on January 1879 an earthquake rocked the tower and for a moment the keeper on watch thought the tower was going to tumble down.

Some of the property around the new lighthouse was government property. Beginning after 1904, the U.S. Navy built a telegraph station to better communicate with shipping. This was abandoned after World War II. Today the U.S. Coastguard maintains the historic light. The keeper's house has become a museum with changing exhibits. A new exhibit opened May 6, 2016.

In 2009 an Archaeological Maritime Program was begun. A wreck dating to 1772 was located in shallow water just south and east of the inlet and today is known as the Storm Wreck. Artifacts fished up from the site have been put on display to help visitors better understand the hardships and rewards of living on a barrier island.

The St. Augustine Lighthouse & Museum is located at 81 Lighthouse Avenue in Lighthouse Park. Various exhibits, both in the keeper's house and on the surrounding grounds, are open from 9 a.m. to 6 p.m. daily. There is an admission fee.

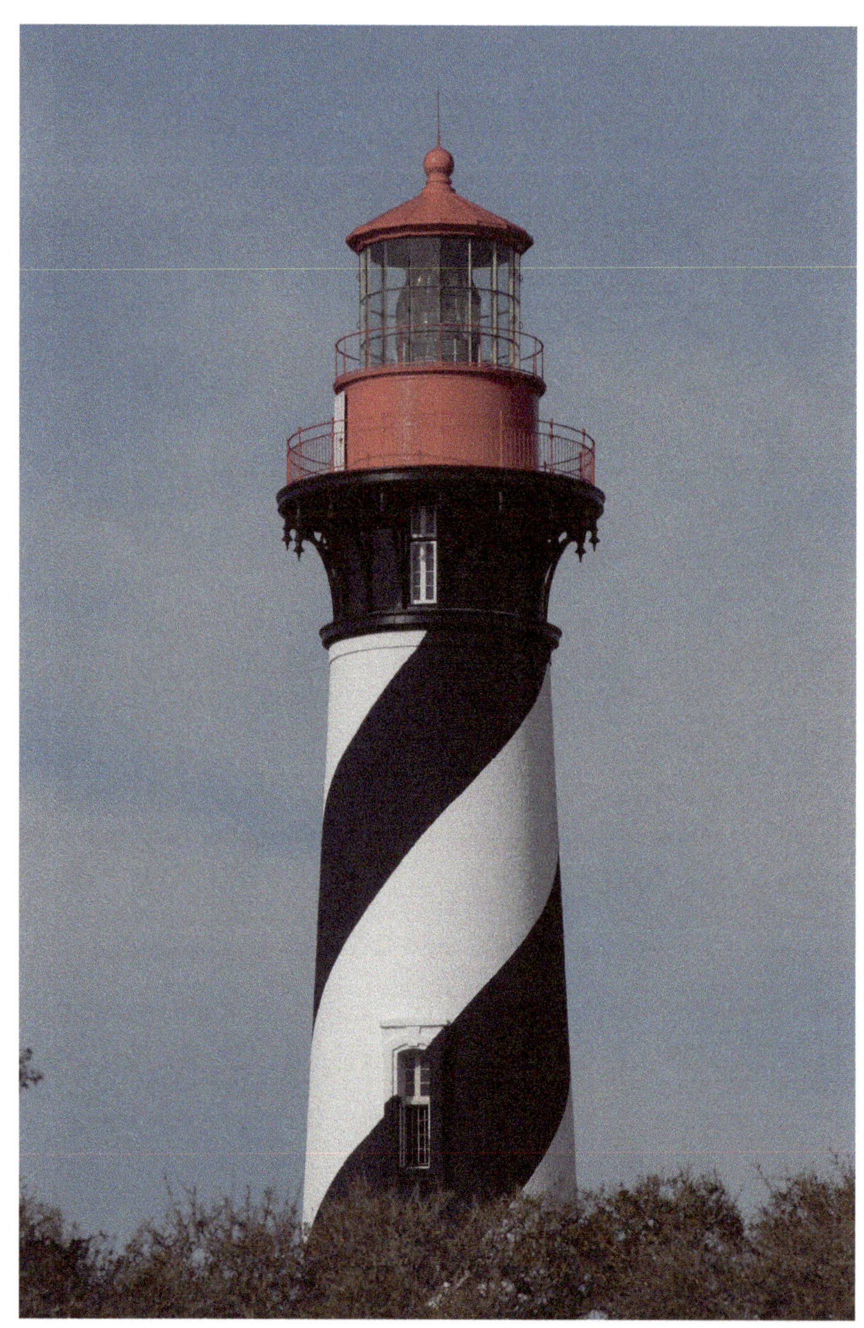

The tower was finished in 1874.

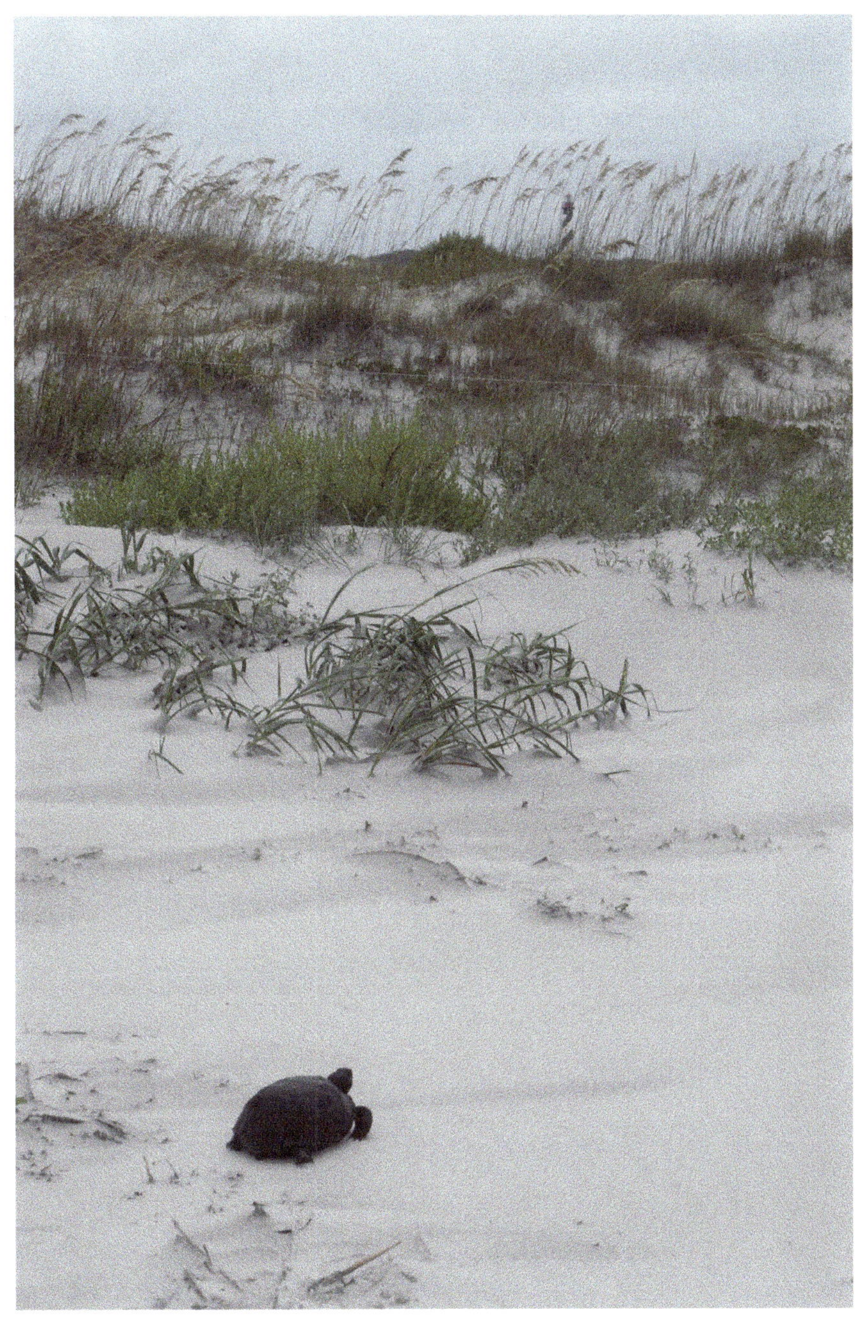

A Gopher Tortoise on Conch Island.

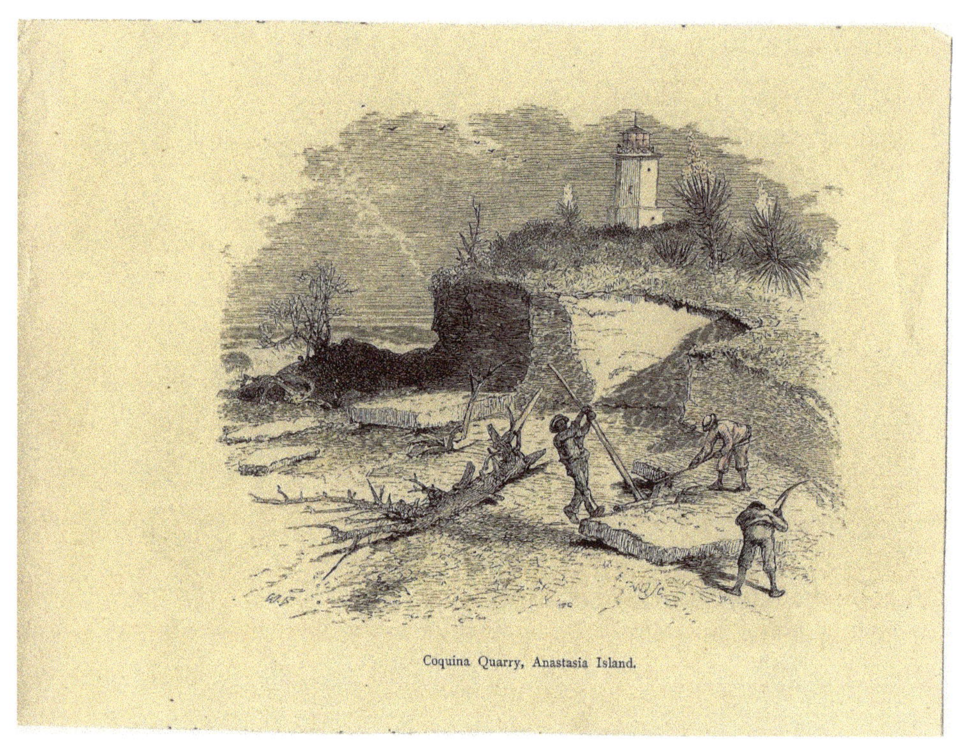

Cutting coquina near the old lighthouse.
From Kenneth M. Barrett, Jr.'s collection.

Anastasia State Park

Just a short walk or ride south of the St. Augustine Lighthouse is Anastasia State Park, 1,500 wind-swept acres bordering the Atlantic Ocean. Camping spots are located within the maritime forest. Wind surfing and kayaking take place inside the salt water lagoon and estuary known as Salt Run.

There is an ancient dune trail for hikers and four miles of beautiful white sand beaches for the beachcomber. Surfing and fishing activities, stand-up paddle boarding, bike riding, and running and walking along the tideline entice visitors and locals alike to get out and enjoy the fresh air.

The long beach and the adjacent sand dunes are products of the hand of man and mother nature. The north end of the beach is named after Florence Edge, a St. Augustine native known as Old Conchie or Conch, who fished and camped on a little island that was there around the turn of the last century. The Army Corps of Engineers dredged the current inlet and built two long jetties back in the 1950s. The north end of the park became known as Conch's Island or Conch Island. The constantly shifting sand bars and shoals added further sand and before long the beach began to build and rebuild itself after hurricanes and northeasters.

St. Augustine Inlet has always been difficult to navigate and the early written records tell of the danger of crossing the bar to get inside the safety of the inlet. Many ships and cargo were lost due to storms or poor navigation. Harbor pilots during Spanish and British periods provided some measure of safety as they helped bring ships into the harbor known as Matanzas Bay.

A barrier island stretching for 14 miles, Anastasia is really a big slab of coquina shell rock that was discovered as early as 1586. Covered with sand and sea oats, Spanish Bayonet, huge old live oak trees, bay and cedar trees, and palmetto and scrub, this ancient shell rock provided the Spanish with coquina stone to build Castillo de San Marcos and other public buildings during the early days. Work was begun in 1672 to uncover these layers of easily cut stone. Exposed to fresh air and sunlight, they hardened into the stone work used to build the old fort, the Cathedral, Government House and other buildings.

In 1765, the colonial naturalist William Bartram visited the coquina quarries and made notes on flora and fauna he found in the area. The large open quarry that became home to the St. Augustine Amphitheatre in 1965 appears in his writing.

In the late Spring thousands of various shorebirds visit the beaches of the park to mate and nest, raising their young birds upon the shoreline. The least tern arrives in May and stays into the summer nesting on the hard shell sand behind the fore dunes. Their unique sound can be heard all over the island. Sanderlings, skimmers and royal terns also nest in the park.

Just inside the entrance to the park is an existing coquina quarry with an interpretive marker and winding trails beneath the oak tree canopy. As one heads south along A1A, the small ponds and lakes indicate other quarries which would eventually fill with water. The quarries south of the lighthouse were filled in by the city beginning in the 1940s. Coquina and St. Augustine go together like milk and sugar.

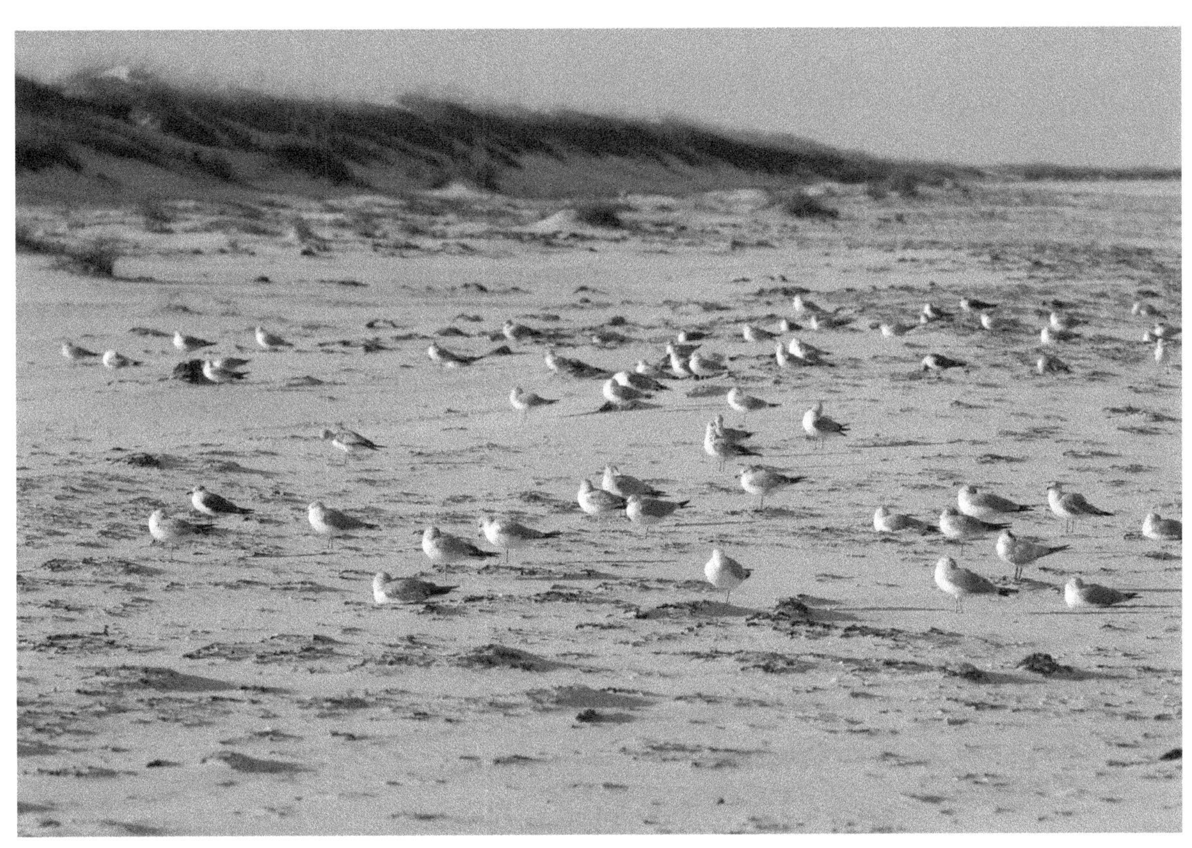

Winter

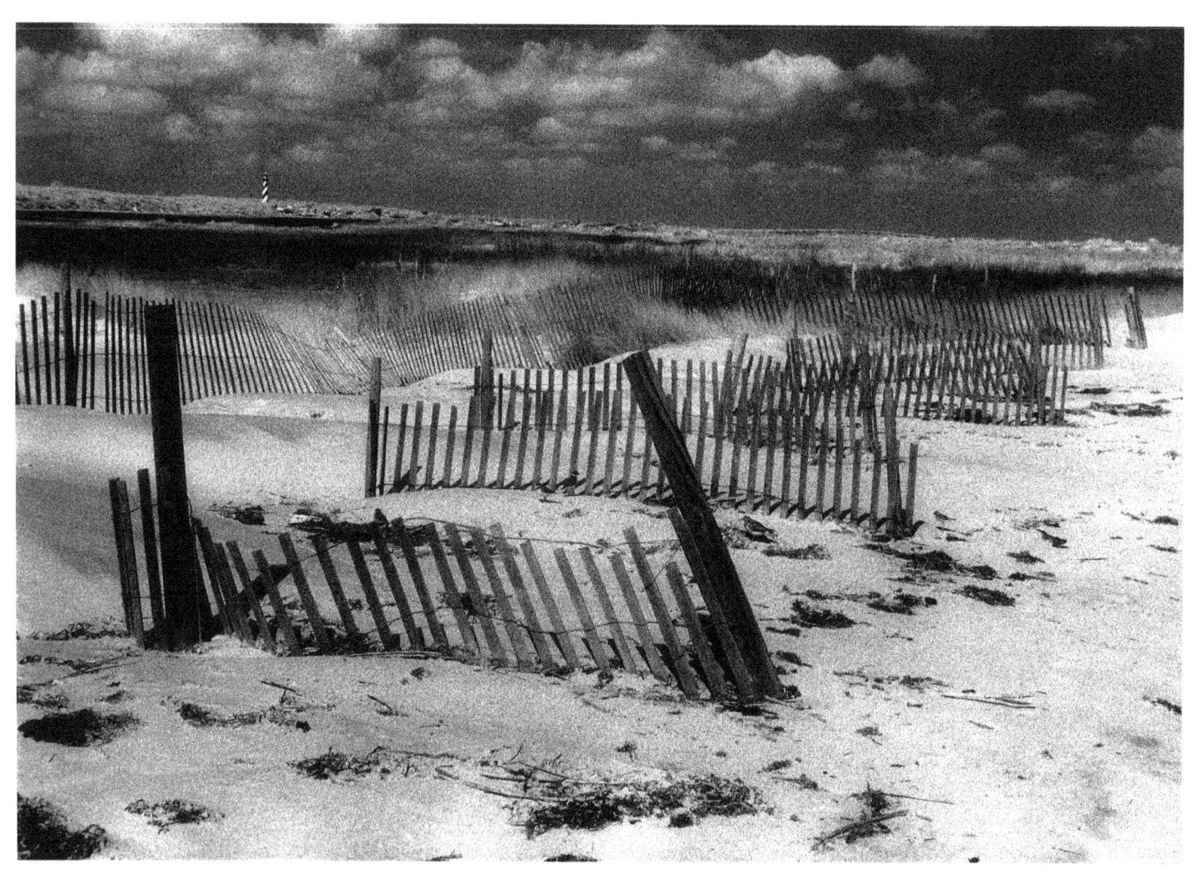

Conch Island black and white infrared.

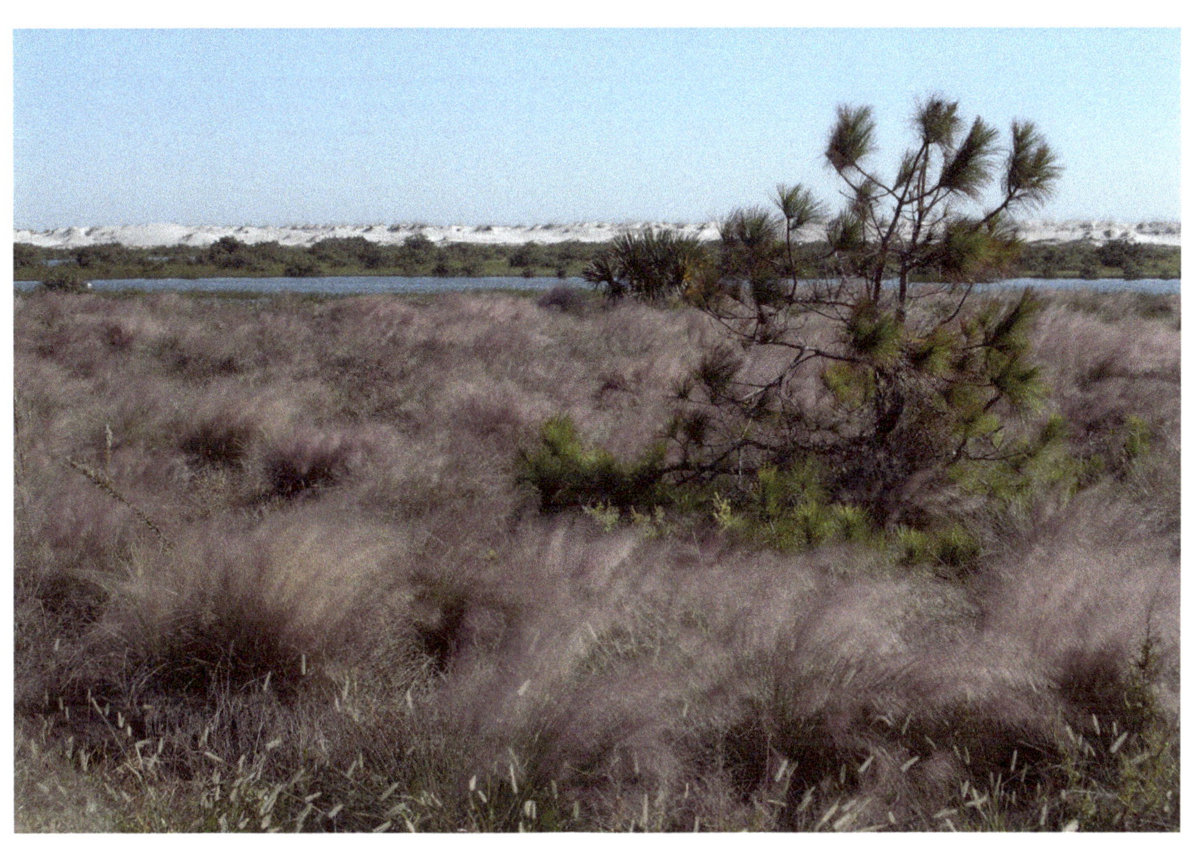

The meadow in Anastasia State Park during Fall.

Dawn

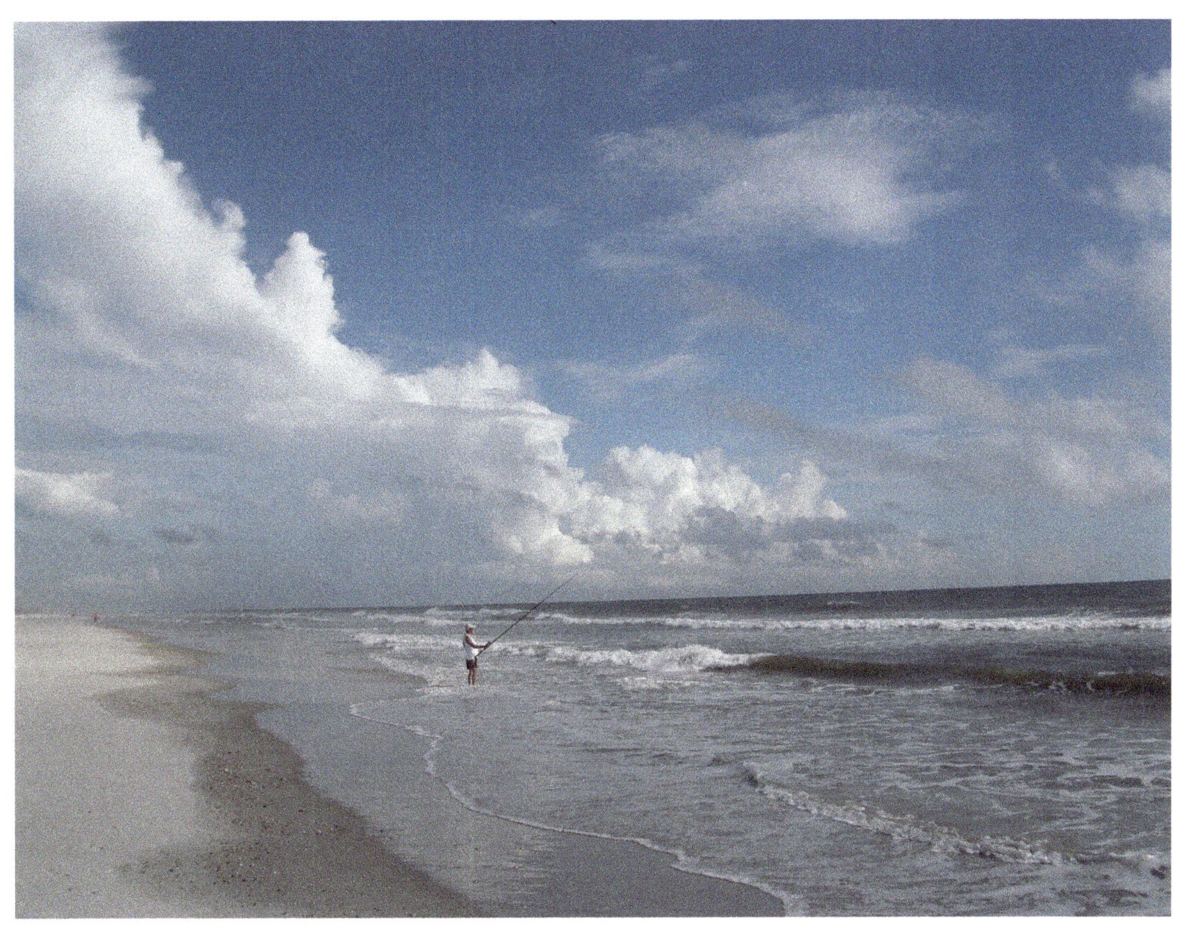

Surf fishing

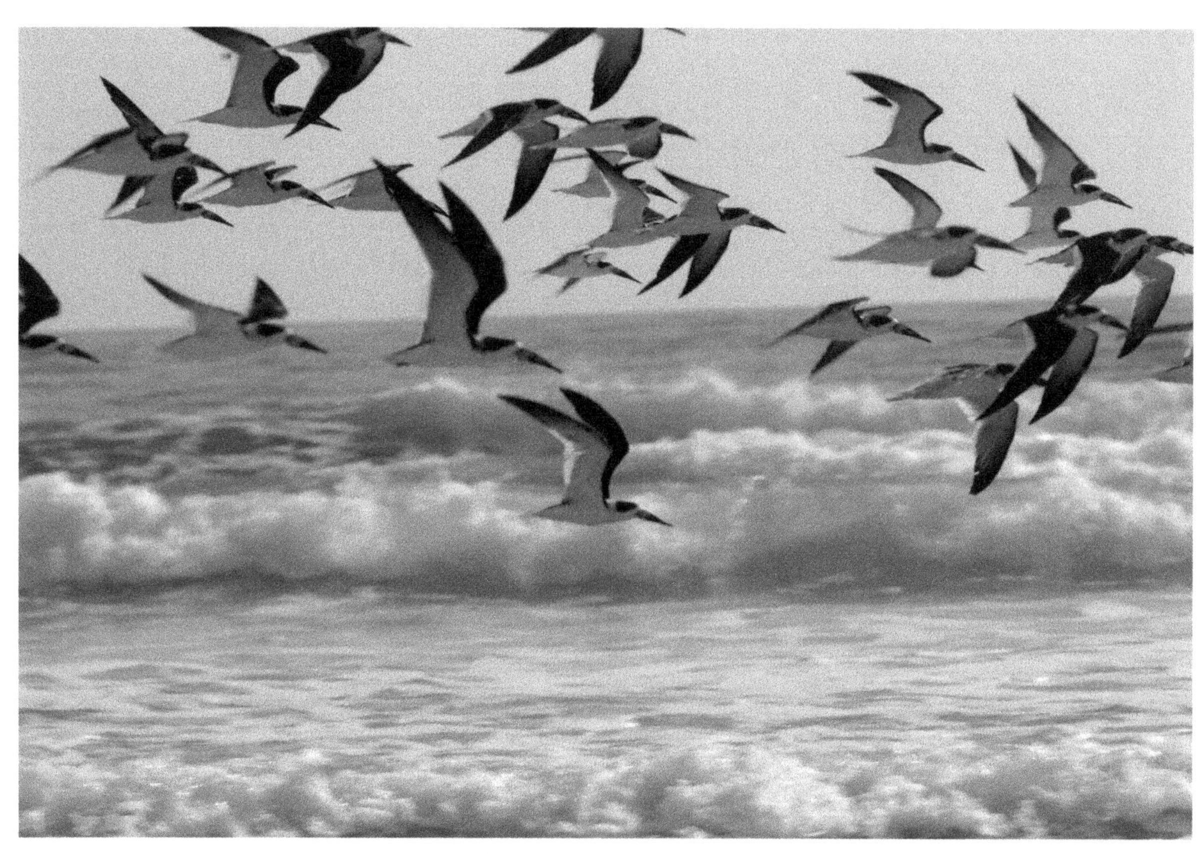

Black Skimmers

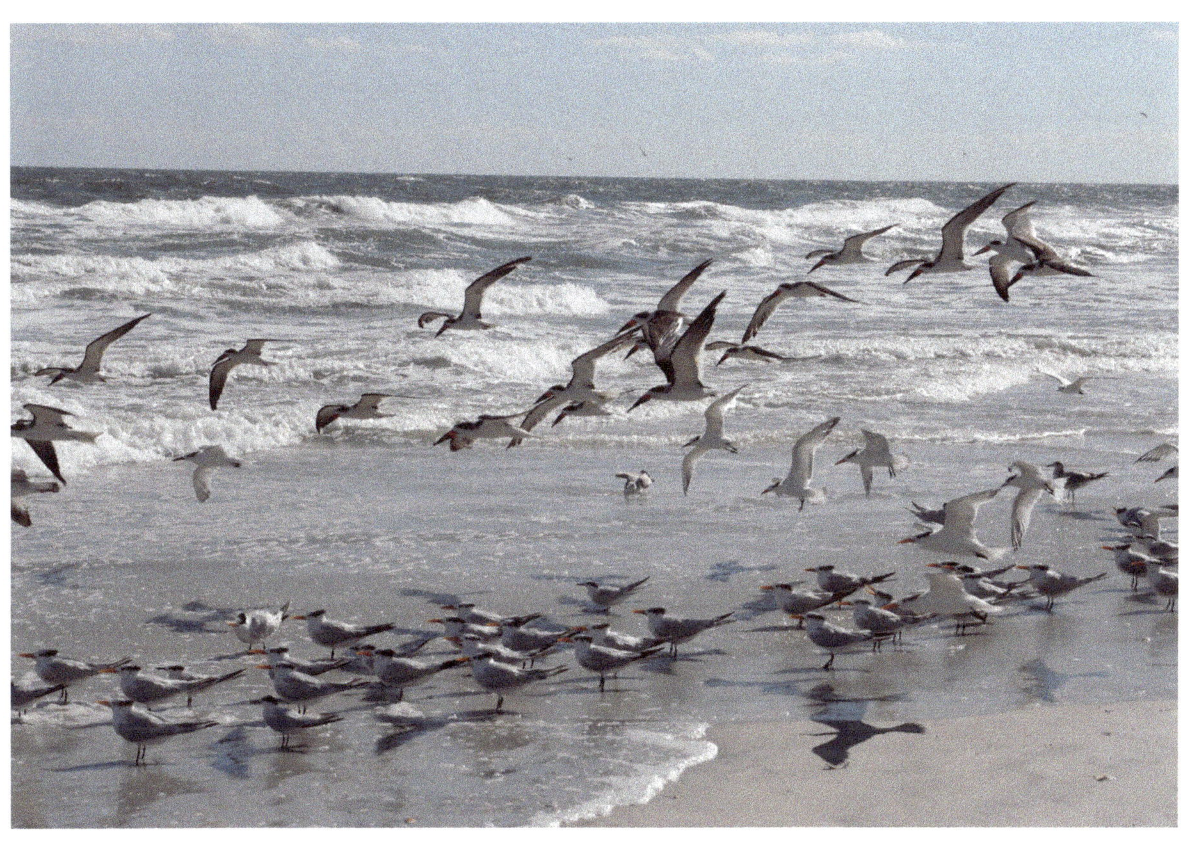

Birds in flight near St. Augustine Inlet.

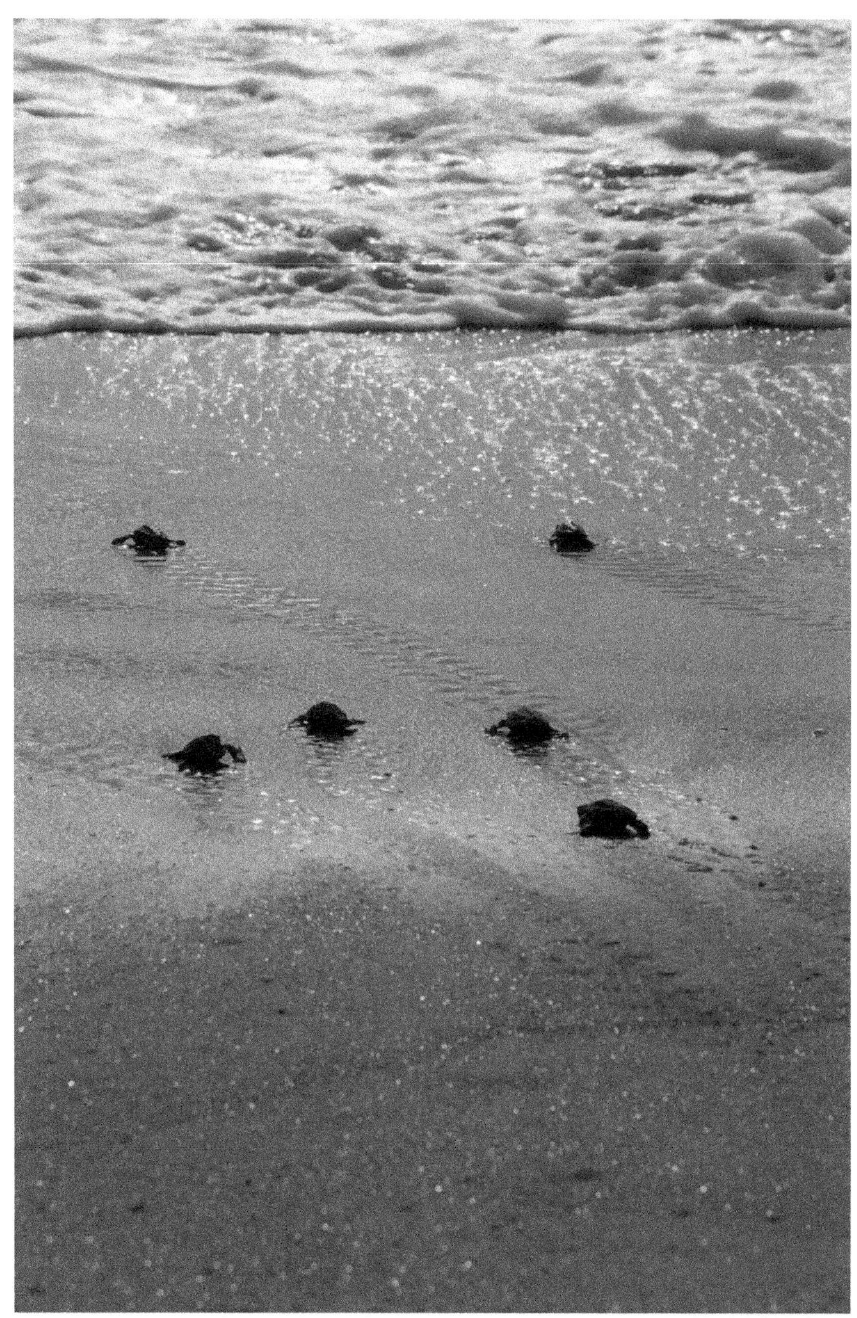

Tiny turtles head for home.

St. Augustine Alligator Farm Zoological Park

Just a short drive or bicycle ride south along State Road A1A from downtown St. Augustine is the St. Augustine Alligator Farm, one of the oldest attractions in Florida. Indians, Spanish settlers and early travel writers were fascinated by these prehistoric creatures.

Founded around 1893, the farm was located at the terminus of the old sandy road that led to South Beach, now St. Augustine Beach. Visitors could board a short-line railway and travel to the St. Augustine Lighthouse and south to a small collection of beach houses and what became a must-see collection of snakes, alligators and marine oddities.

Located on the shores of the Atlantic Ocean, one could wander through the various displays of reptiles and marine themed exhibits. A dance hall was built to provide entertainment in the evening. If you wanted to stay the night, you could rent a small cottage on the beach and thrill to the sound of the crashing surf. The collection of alligators continued to grow to several hundred.

By the early 1920s, the shoreline was eroding along the eastern tideline. A series of storms and nor'easters threatened to wash away the beach. Fires burned some of the beach houses and the dance hall. The railway was washed out during one powerful storm. Fire also swept through the Alligator Farm buildings and the farm was relocated to its present location after 1921. Fire again burned the wooden buildings at the new location on A1A and the present building was constructed after 1937.

The now familiar mission-style building faces A1A and thousands of visitors enjoy the alligator pens, a boardwalk across the marsh and numerous exhibits. During the early months of spring, thousands of birds build their nests above the alligators' home to raise their young. Spoonbills, curlews, egrets, ibis and herons attract birdwatchers and photographers.

Today, the idea of a "farm" of alligators is a throwback to the past. While there are indeed hundreds of gators, there are also crocodiles, a rookery of birds that nest in the hammock overhanging the marshes, and educational exhibits that help explain the complex nature of Florida's wildlife.

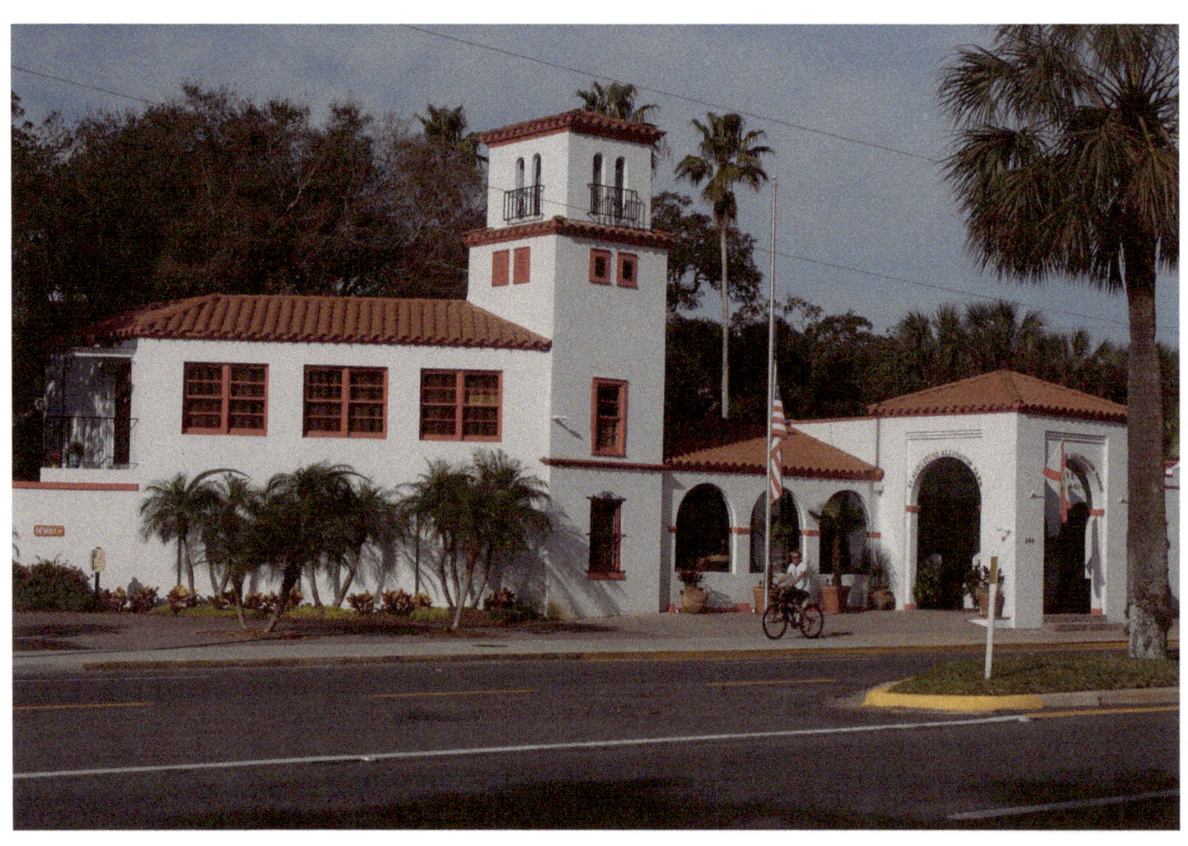

St. Augustine Alligator Farm

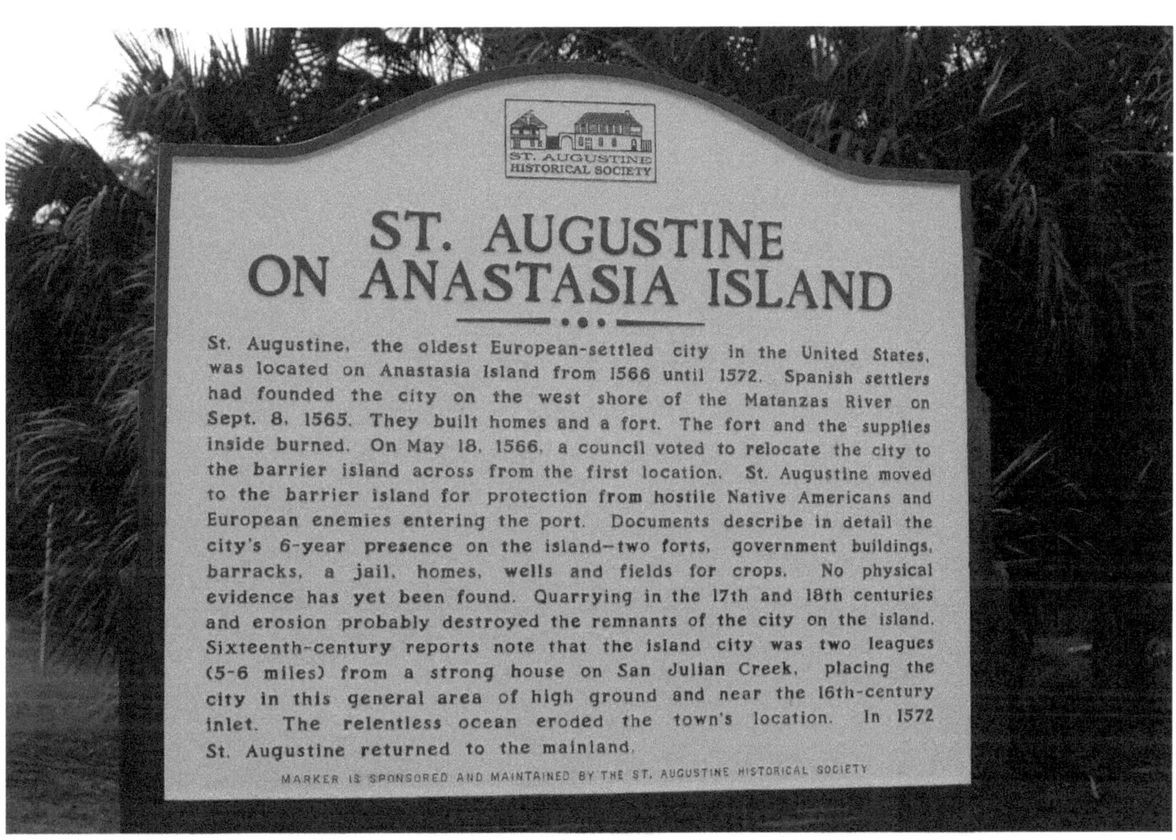

Newest historical marker on the island dedicated Summer 2016.

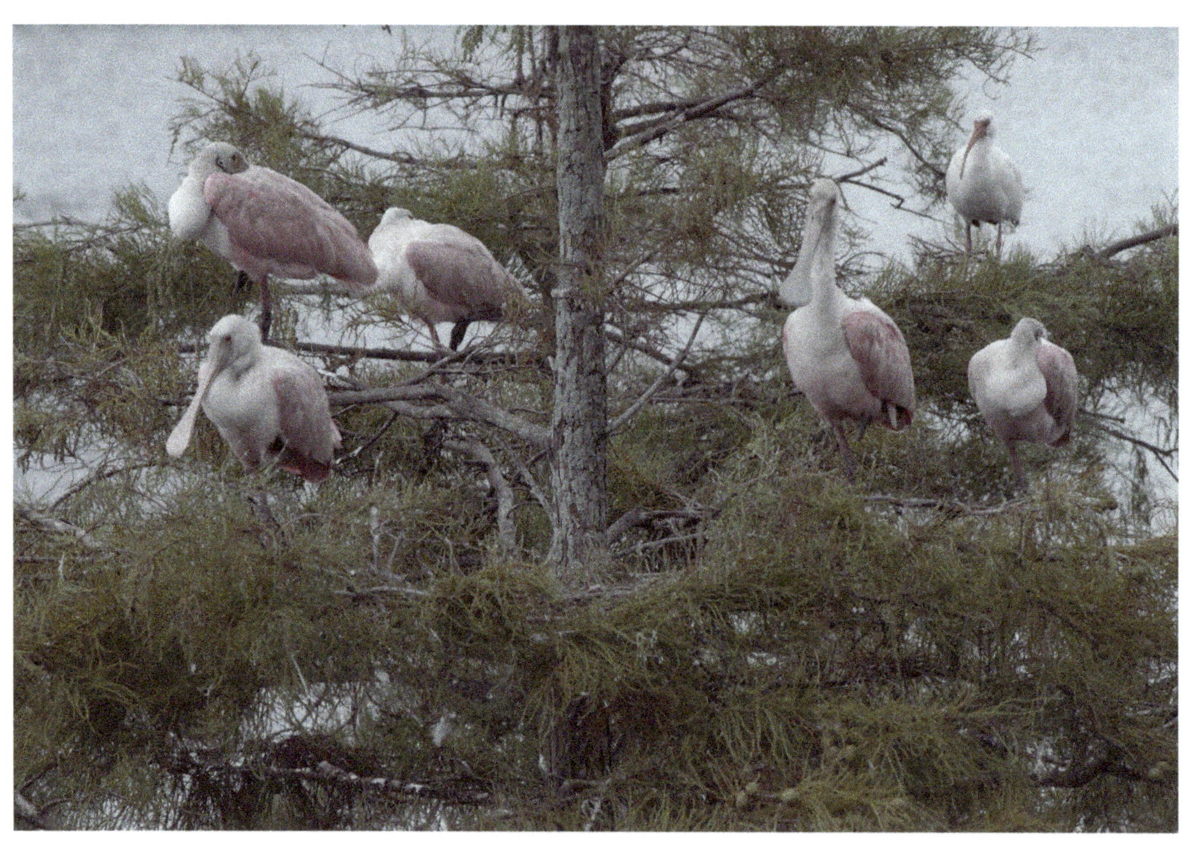

Roseate Spoonbills

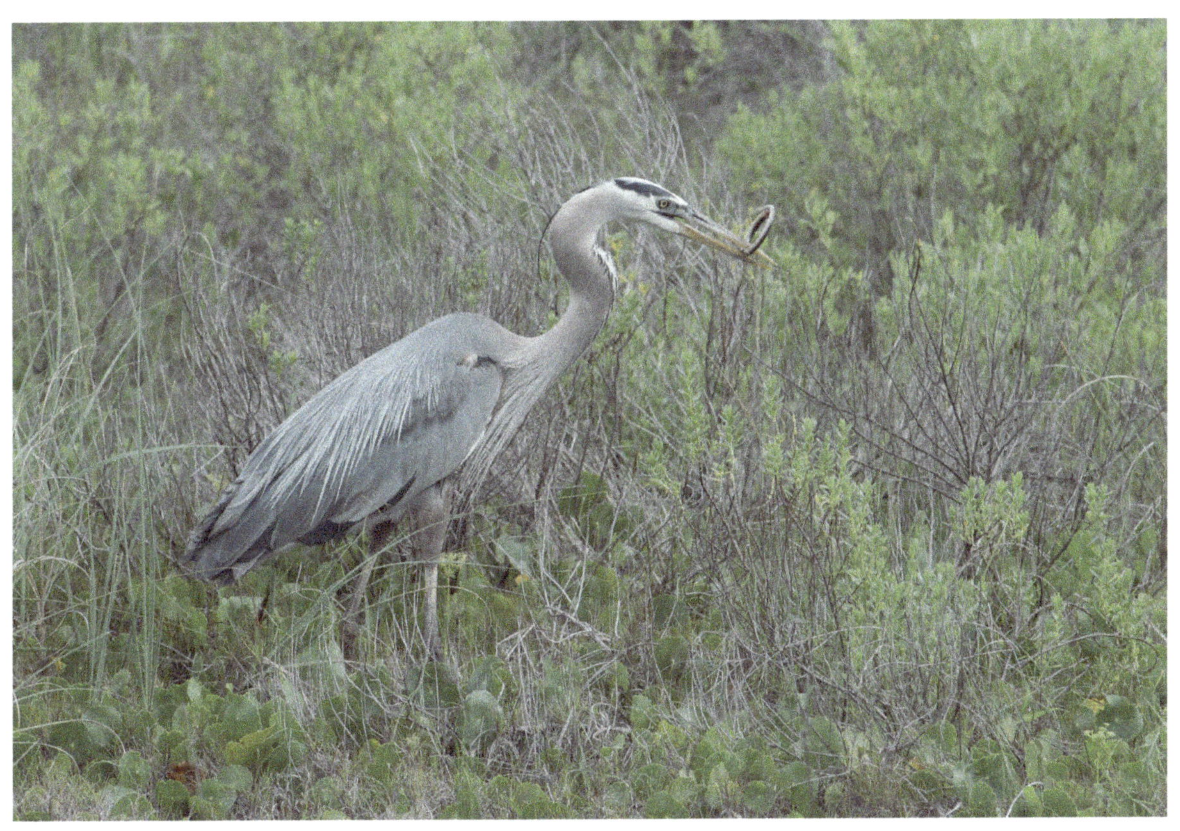

Great Blue Heron

Old Spanish Chimney and Well

Just south of the lighthouse on Old Beach Road, the remains of an old chimney and well mark the site of the master mason's residence. Historian Charles Arnade mentions in his 1961 publication, The Architecture of Spanish St. Augustine, that the building was occupied by the foreman of the work-crew employed in quarrying coquina blocks.

Standing on a ridge of coquina today, surrounded by red cedar trees, the remains of the chimney suggest that the original First Spanish Period building was a rather large structure. No drawings or plans have been found to depict it. Preparation of daily meals and warming in the cold months took place here. It would have been a place for the workers to rest and sleep when not employed in cutting stone.

In 1975, St. Johns County put up an historic marker naming the foreman or overseer as Alonso Diaz Mejia. There is no mention how long he might have stayed here, if he had family in town or where he might have been from originally. The private residence south of this spot sits on property covered with bits and pieces of pottery, cast-off coquina and relics from those who camped out in this isolated location. Archeological investigation reveals Spanish workers were living here when the Castillo de San Marcos was under construction, 1672-1695.

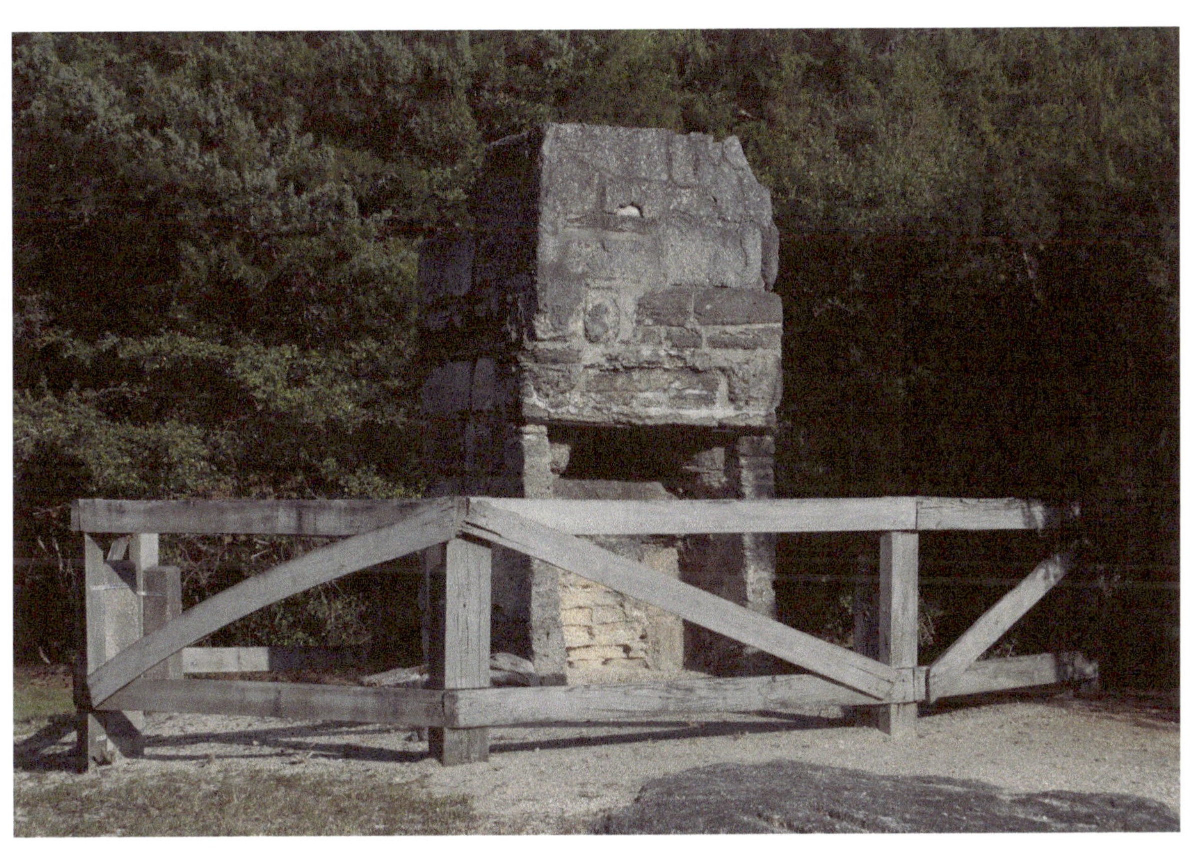

Old Spanish Chimney

Lakeside Park

Old Beach Road in the old days connected Lighthouse Park with St. Augustine Beach, known as South Beach until the early 1900s. Lakeside Park, founded in 2005, sits on the south dead end of Old Beach Road even though it has an A1A address.

Just east of the highway it faces Lake Anhinga. The lake at one time was part of the quarries that stretched south of the lighthouse. Over time, the quarries would fill with water and the masons and stone cutters would move to a new location. During low tide, it is easy to see the coquina sloping down into the water's edge.

In this little park stands the Veterans Memorial Sculpture Garden. The Veterans Memorial was dedicated in November 2009 and honors "For those who have fought for it, freedom has a flavor the protected will never know." It is dedicated to all the Armed Forces of the United States.

In June 2011, the Sculpture Garden was installed. The collection of stone figures depicting native Indians and nature were sculpted by Marianne Lerbs, Thomas Glover W. and other artists and installed in the natural areas fronting the little lake. A marker on each describes the name of the piece and the maker.

Despite the highway passing closely by, there is a remarkable quietness and serenity in this lovely little park. Visitors sitting on benches can overlook the lake and its many waterfowl. Fishermen cast a line out hoping for a strike. And if one is patient enough, an anhinga will surface in the lake with a mullet in its beak.

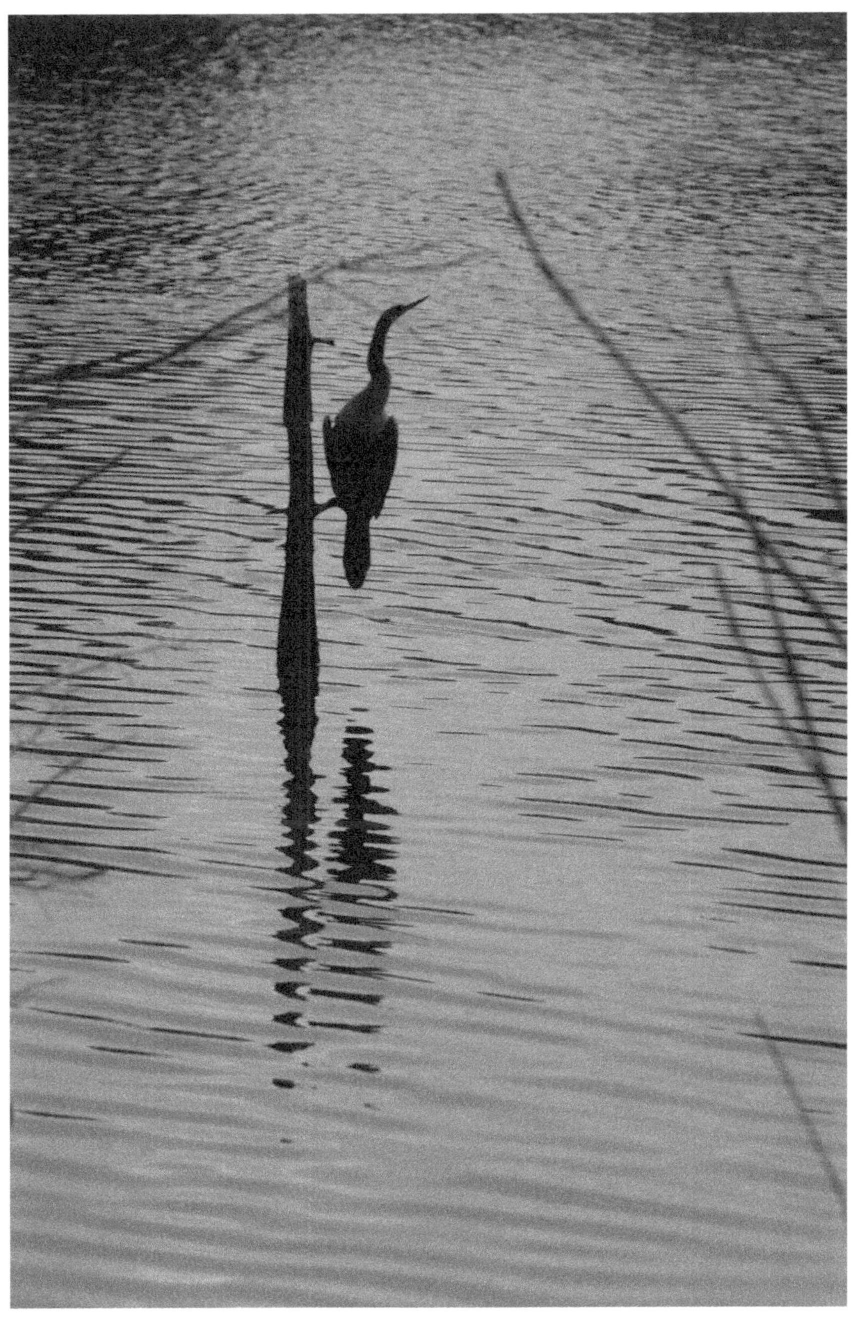

Anhinga

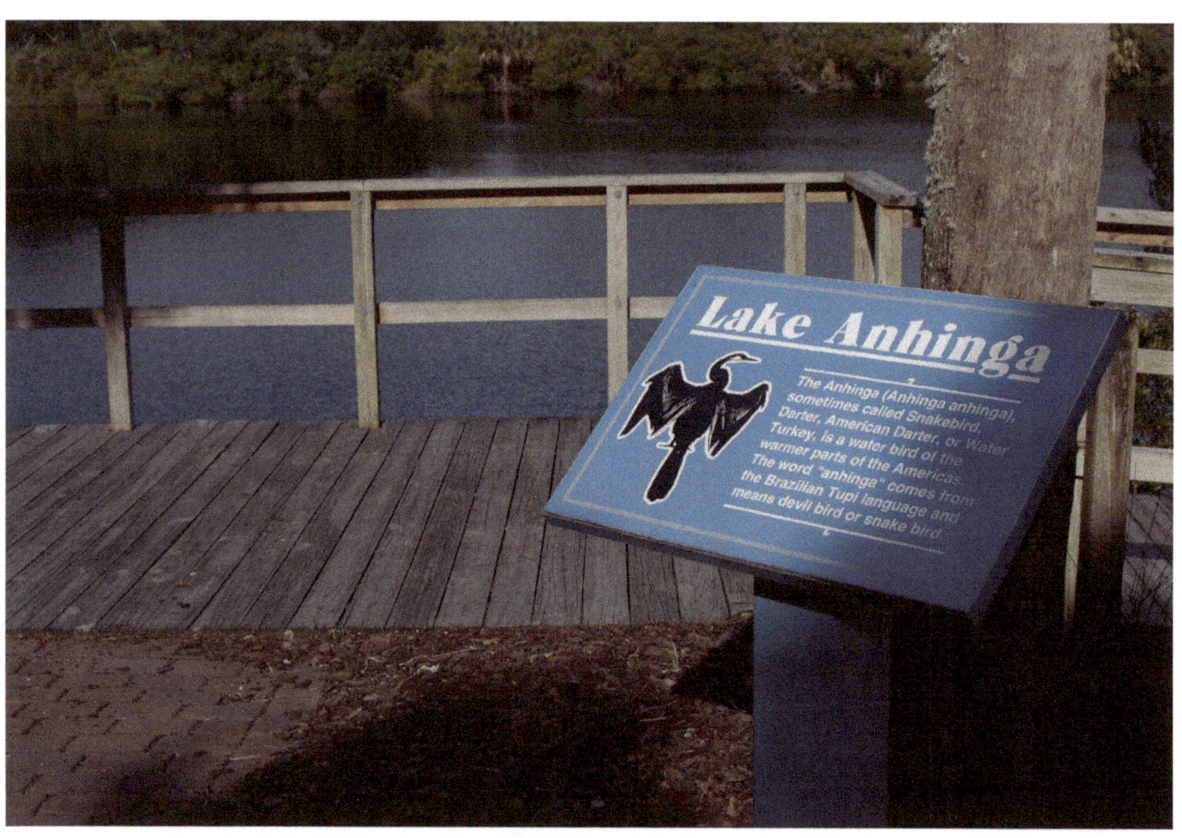

Lake Anhinga

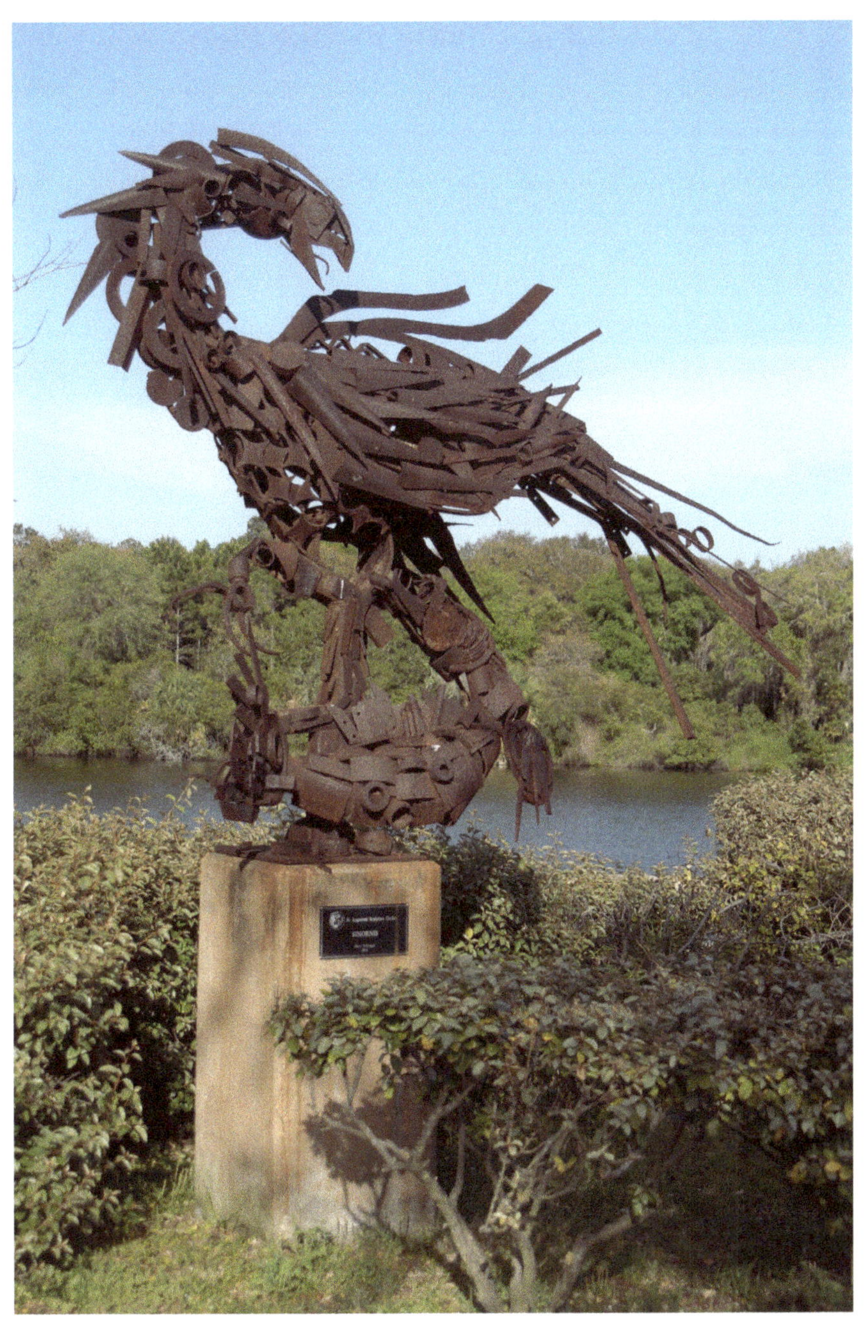

Sculpture Garden

St. Johns County Fishing Pier

The current county fishing pier at St. Augustine Beach was built by Mizner Marine of Tampa, Florida, after the replacement pier was washed away by a storm back in the early1980s. It is the only beachside fishing pier. It also attracts surfers, beachgoers and tourists.

The original pier opened in 1939 and was a Works Progress Administration (WPA) project. It was the first real development in St. Augustine Beach, which had been a tourist spot since the late 1800s, then known as South Beach. The pier area was anchored by two hotels on the north and south sides of the seawall which were built by the county. Various arcades and shops attracted visitors. There was a bandstand and small carnival area. In later years, a drive-in movie theater was founded directly across the west side on State Road A1A.

Hurricanes and northeasters damaged the old wooden pier many times in its almost fifty-year history. Hurricane Dora in 1964 and Hurricane Donna in 1969 did extensive damage to the structure, washing away parts of it during each storm. For a while in the early 1960s, it was the location of civil rights protests, and provided quite a backdrop for photographers who recorded the fighting and protesting. In the late 1960s, it was the place to go for surfing in the St. Augustine area, attracting surfers up and down the east coast. Hurricane David in 1979 washed out the old pier.

Officials tore down the old bandstand, the hotel on the north corner and most recently, a small coquina office on the south side. The hotel on the south side was renovated and serves as headquarters for The Dance Company and an art gallery.

Today there is a pavilion and a splash park for children. Bait and tackle can be found in the small shop at the entrance to the pier. The St. Augustine, Ponte Vedra & the Beaches Visitors and Convention Bureau also has a small shop displaying brochures, maps and publications listing attractions, restaurants and historic sites on the island. On Wednesday mornings, there is a farmer's market from 8 a.m. to 12:30 p.m. Fireworks blast off from the end of the pier on New Year's Eve.

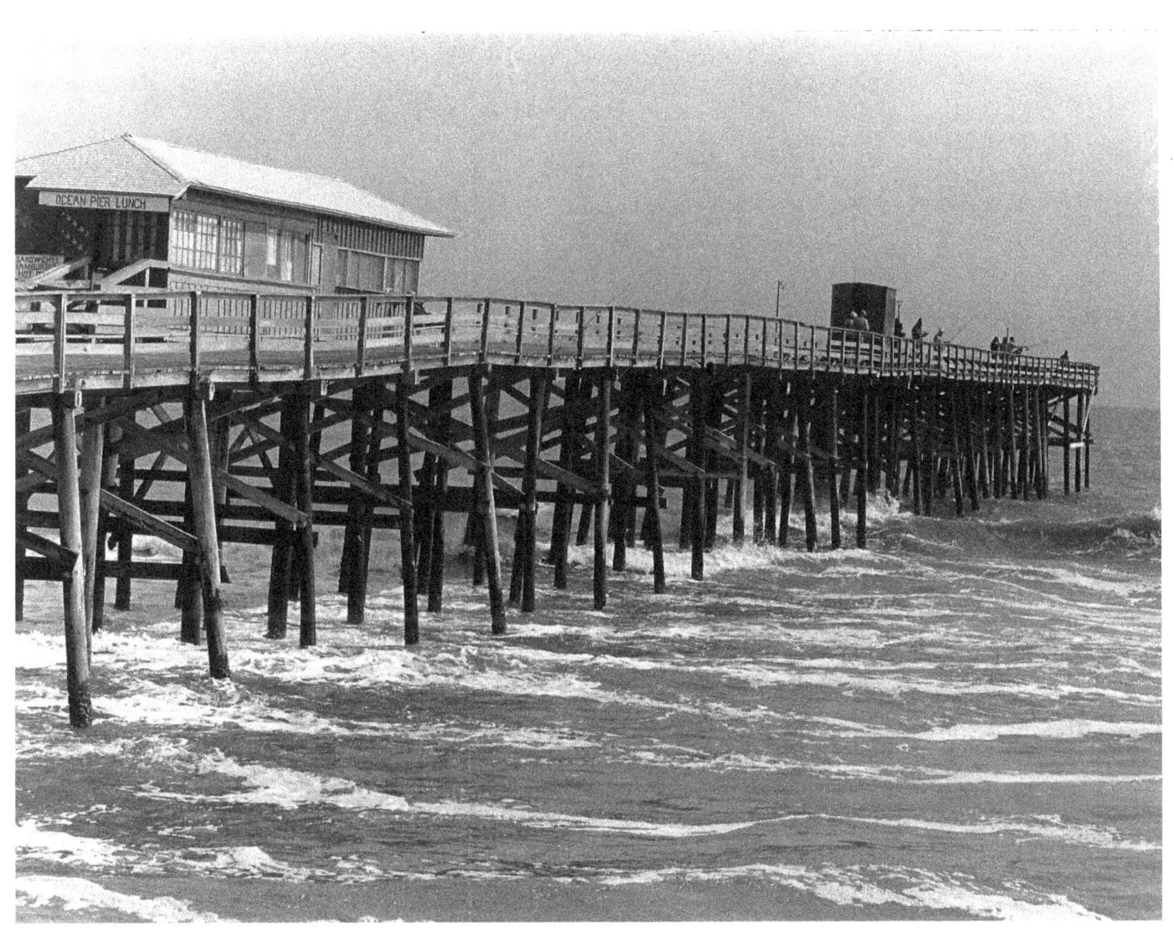

St. Johns County Fishing Pier, 1976

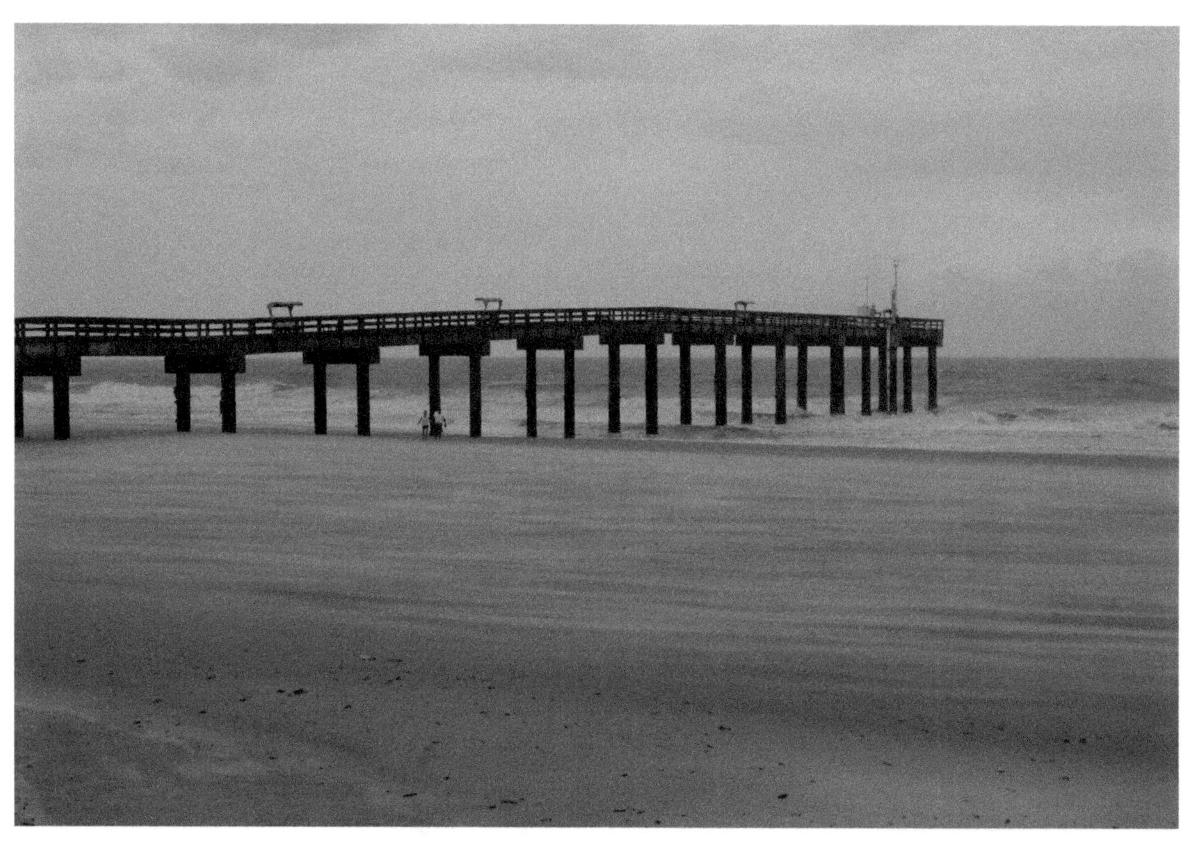

Nor'easter conditions

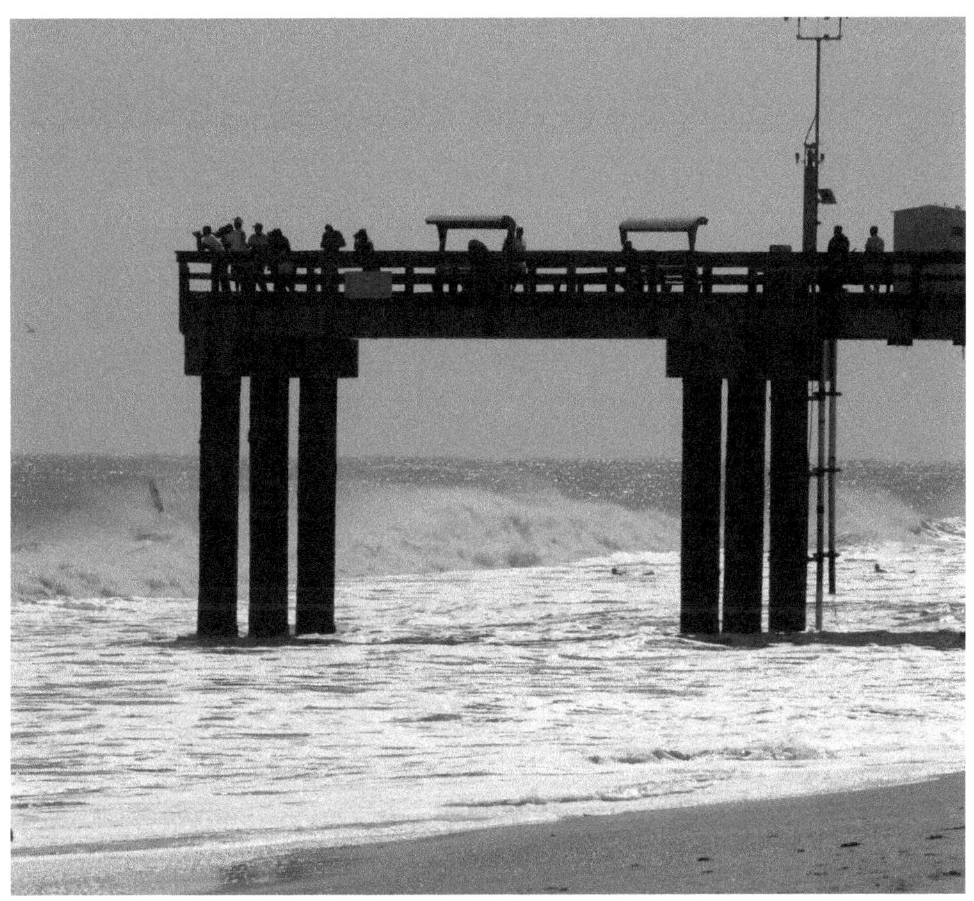

A popular vantage point and fishing spot.

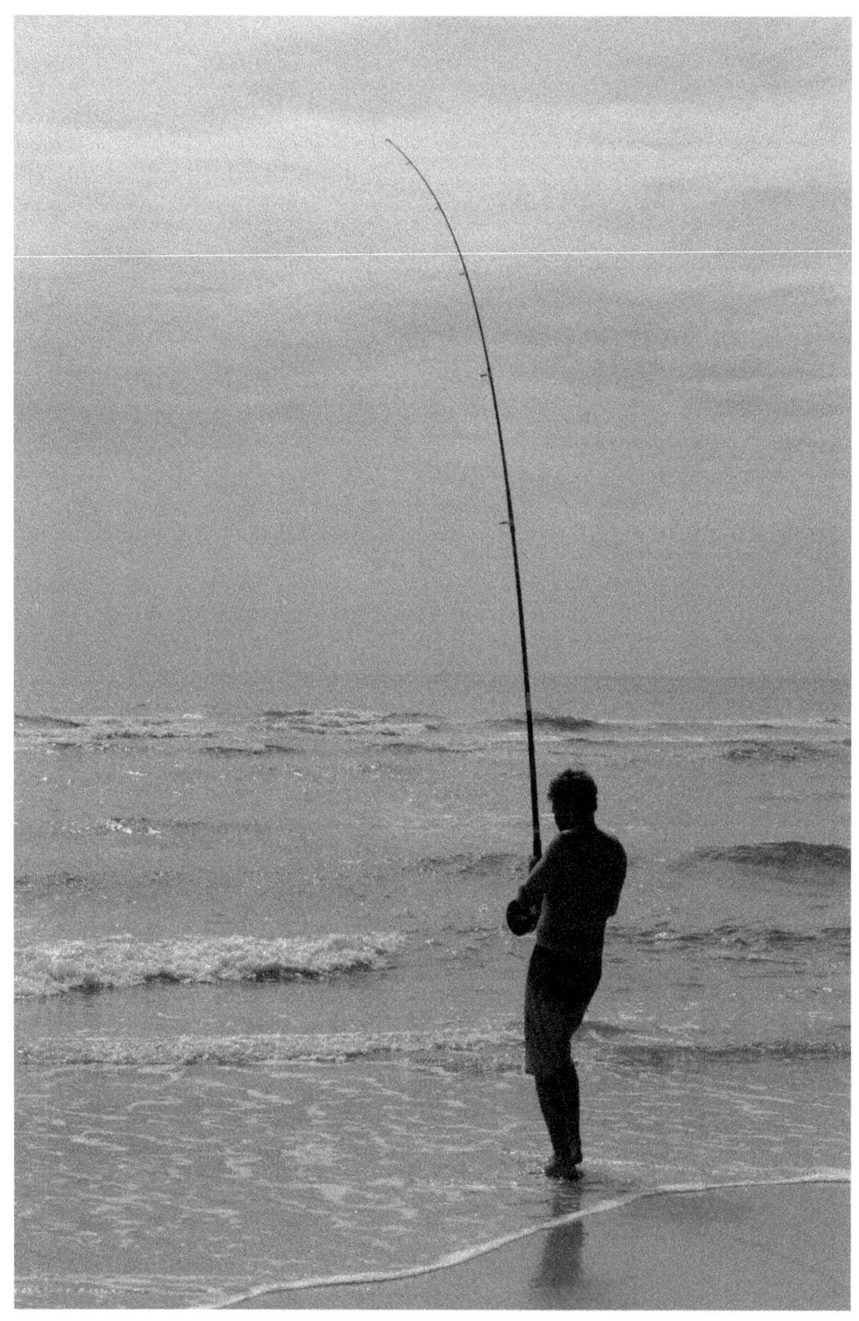

Surf fishing

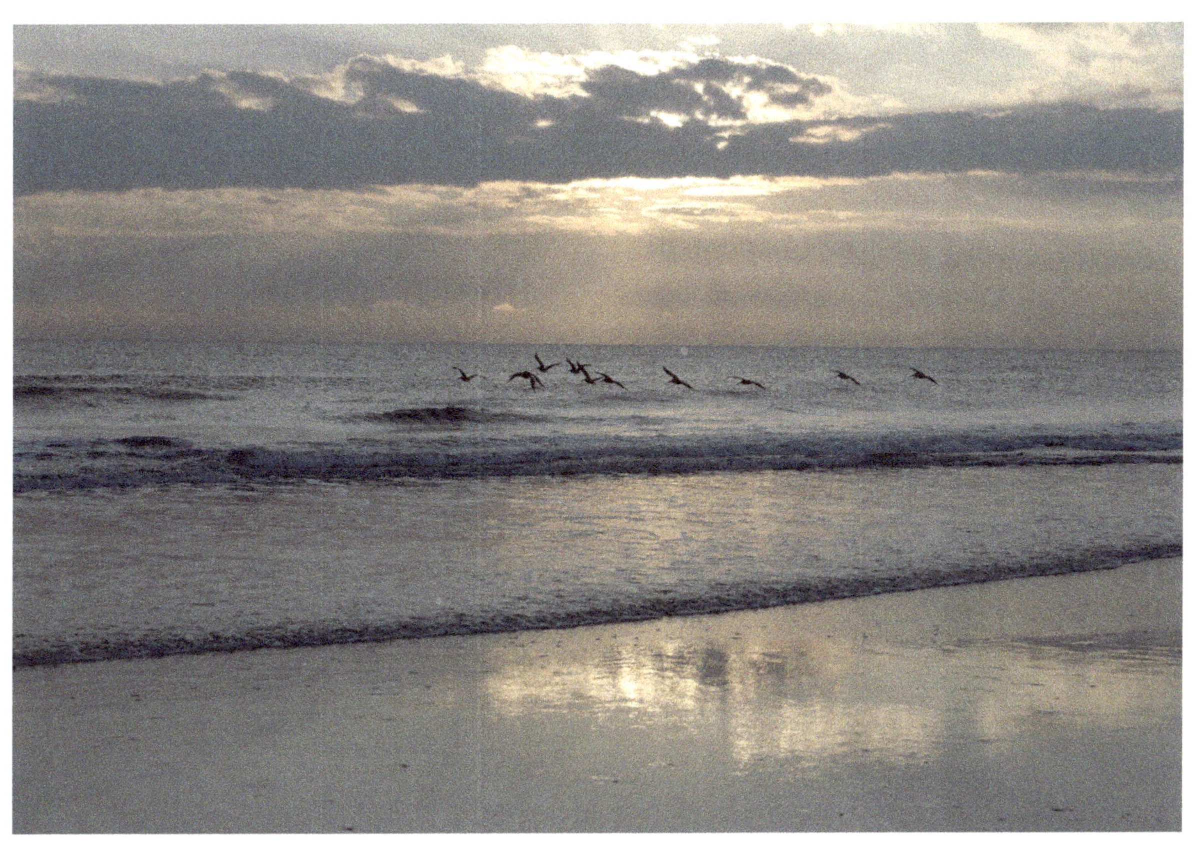

Sunrise

Butler Beach and Crescent Beach

Butler Beach and Crescent Beach could be kindred cousins or siblings.

If you want to know how Crescent Beach received its name, visit the St. Augustine Beach Pier; $3 to fish, $1 to sightsee, and look south down the coastline. As the beach recedes into the distance, it forms a crescent as the sand accumulates along the shore.

Those who built cottages and houses along the strand in the early days used the beach for access as the highway had not yet been constructed. Water was provided by wells and there was no electricity. Old-timers and longstanding residents speak of the quiet beauty of the area and the fact that everyone knew each other.

Completion of State Road 140 (A1A) opened the little community to others. A bridge spanning the Matanzas River brought more visitors from Gainesville and Palatka. Electricity and county water improvements made life easier.

In 1939, noted author Marjorie Kinnan Rawlings bought a small cottage built by one of the founders of Marineland. She had it enlarged sometime later and entertained her friends from the literary world in her Crescent Beach home when she wasn't living in Cross Creek, Florida.

During the same period, well-known St. Augustine businessman Frank Butler and a few partners purchased property from Edgar Pomar to develop what would become Butler Beach, a beachside resort for African-Americans who lived in the Lincolnville community of St. Augustine.

Some of the residents grumbled about this activity, but over time, Butler built a beach bath house, carnival for the kids, a restaurant and small motel. He announced and advertised the opening of the "Sea Breeze Kaseno – the new Colored Recreation Center." Beach activities, fishing, and boating were enjoyed both along the beach and the Matanzas River on the west side. Butler changed the history of the area and St. Augustine by promoting his beachside resort.

The turmoil during the Civil Rights era of the 1960s caused Butler to eventually deed his property to the state. Today there is a county park named for him on the east and west side of State Road A1A. A public boat ramp and picnic pavilions overlook the Matanzas River. Beach access and public parking face the Atlantic Ocean.

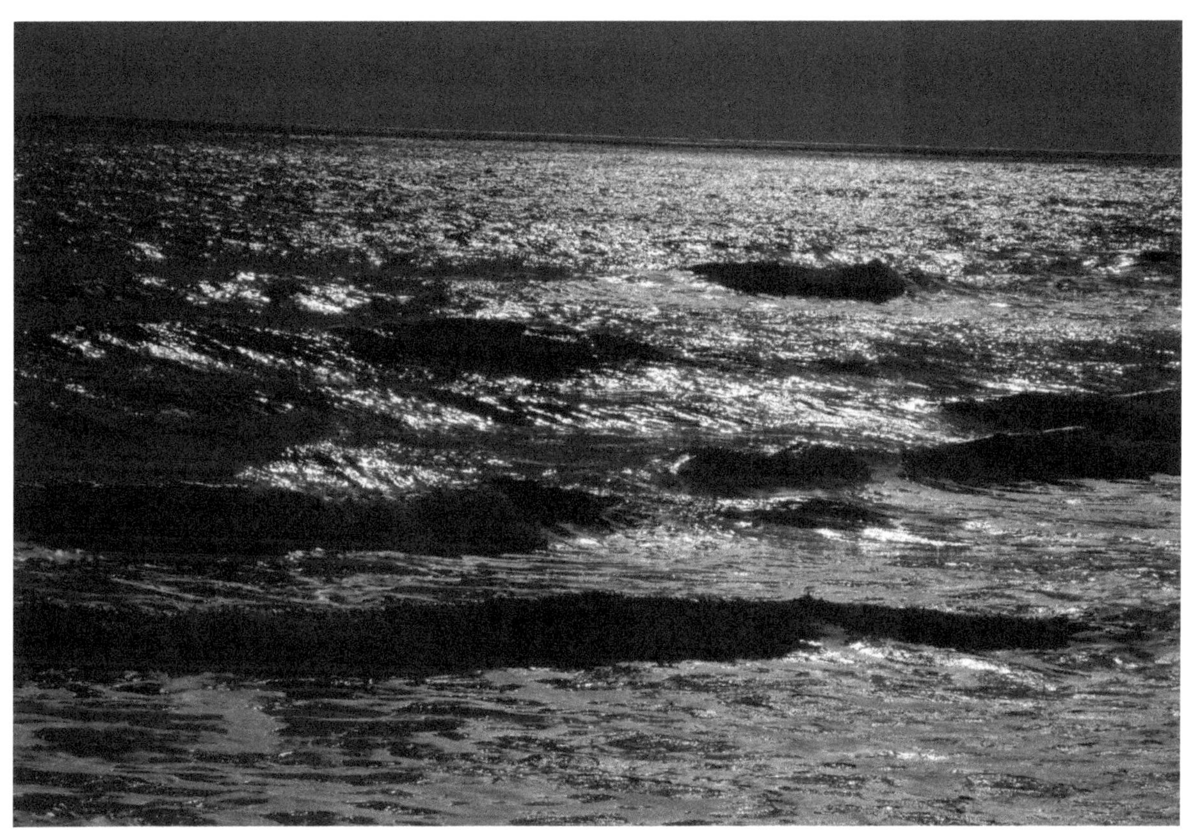

Crescent Beach

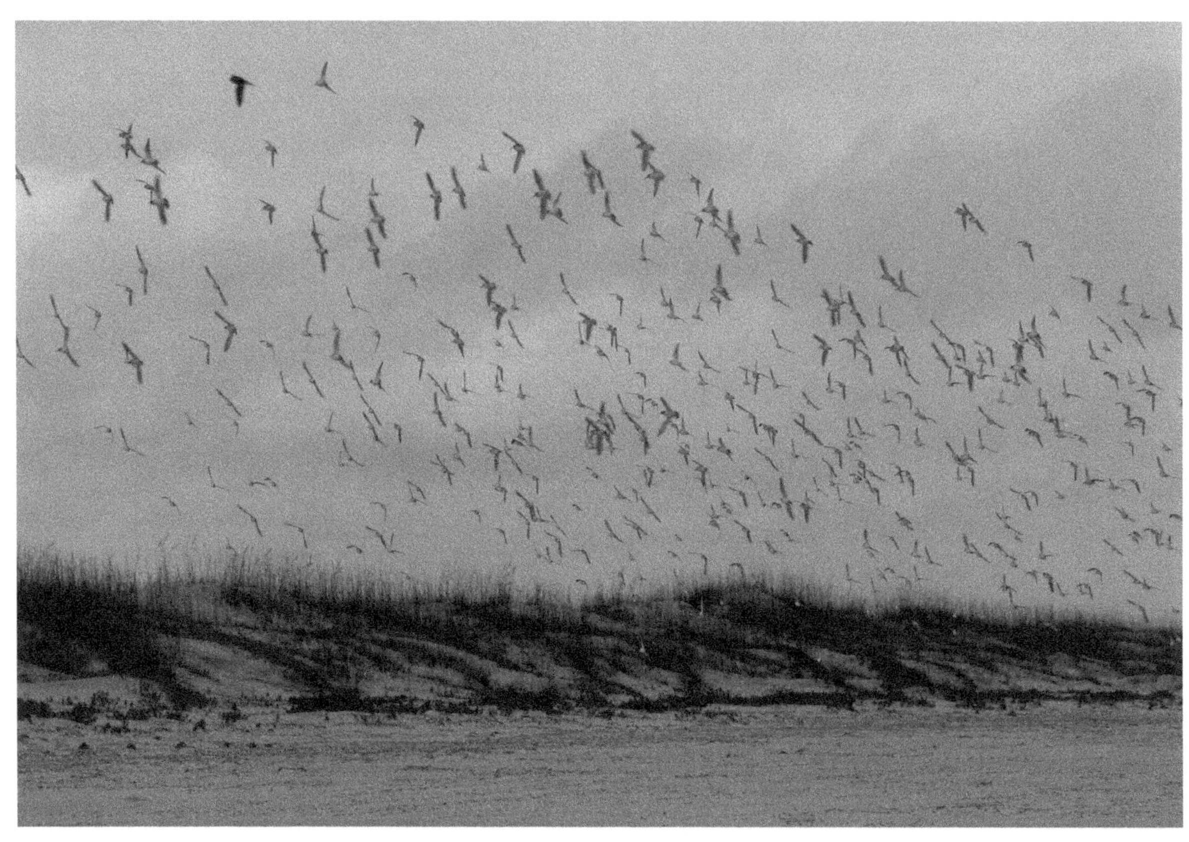

Birds banking in a northeast wind

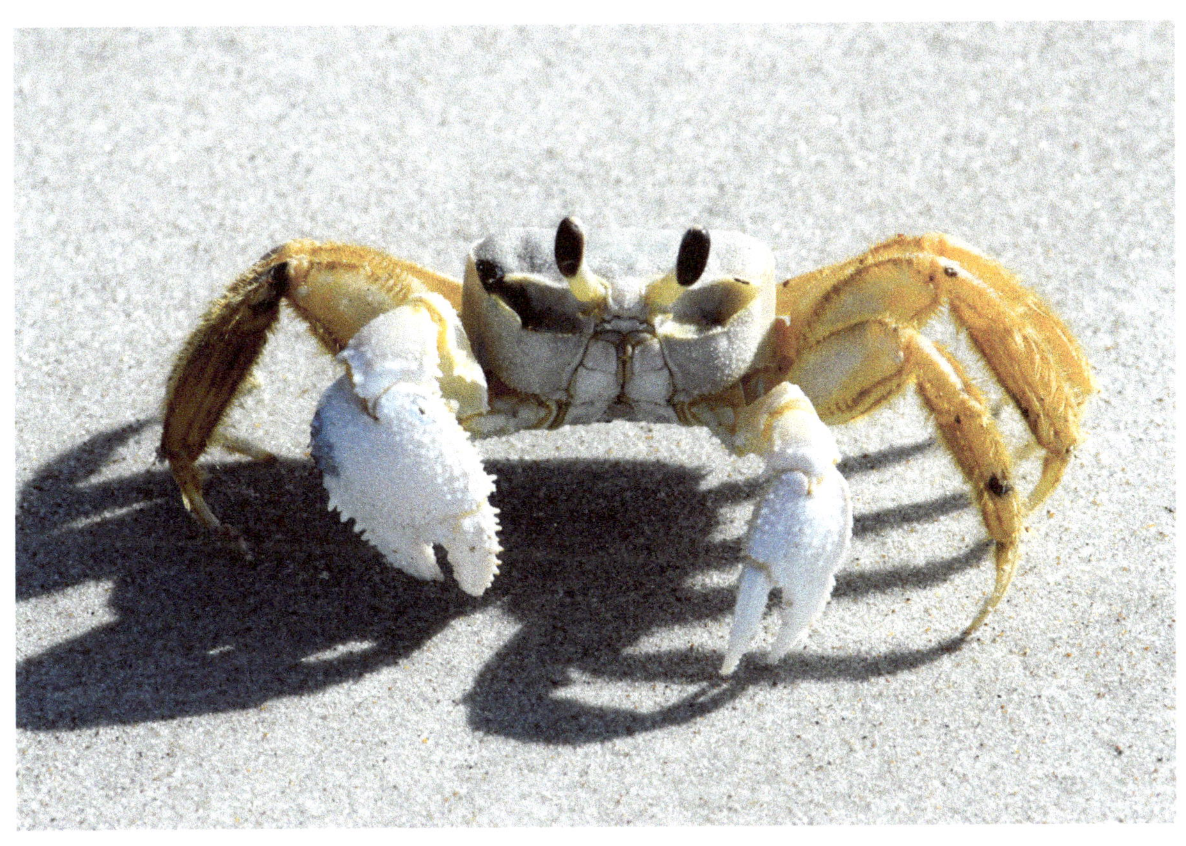

Atlantic Ghost Crab

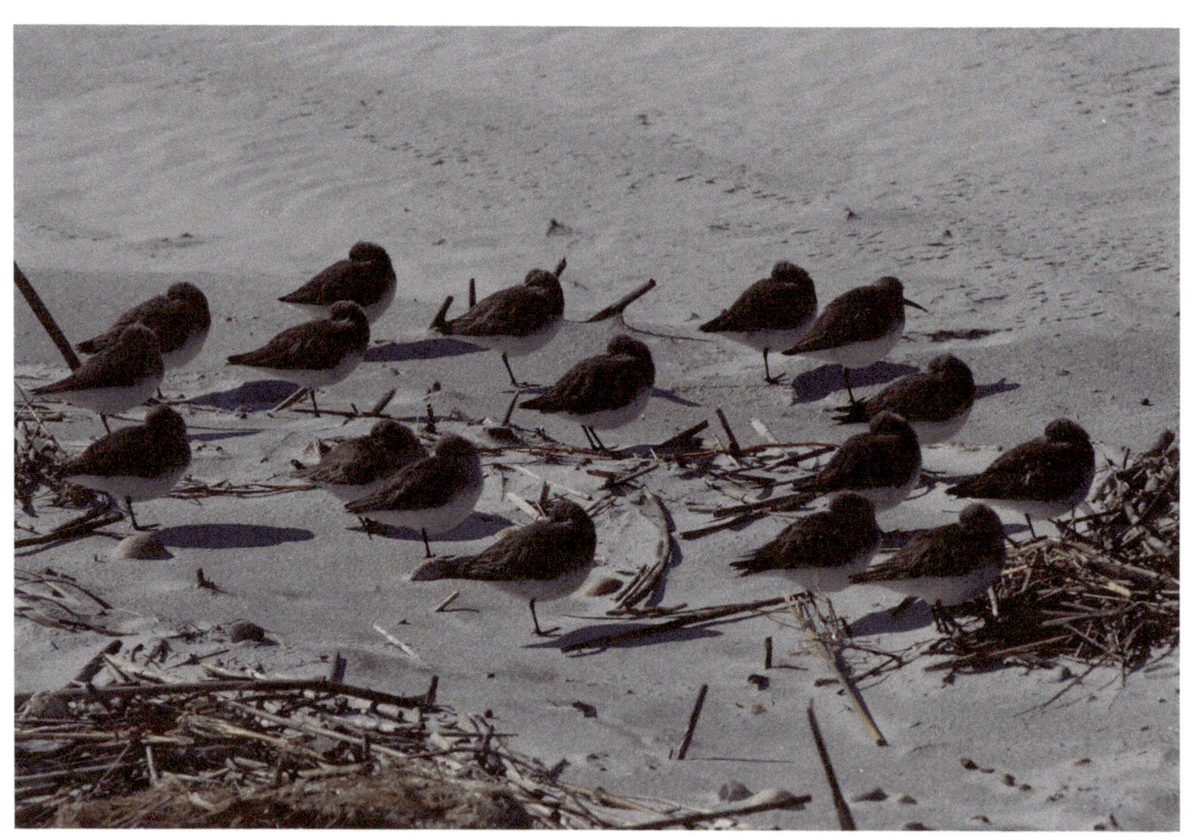

Sandpipers

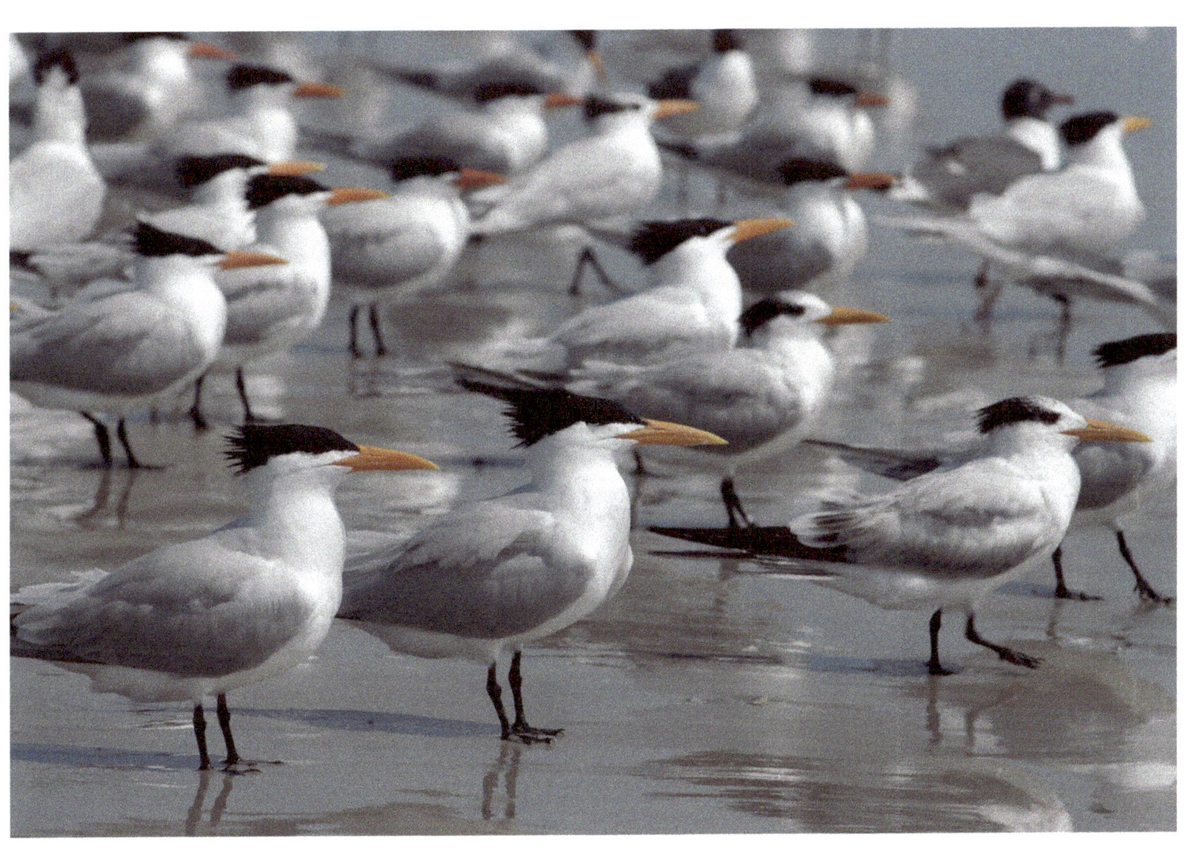

Royal Terns

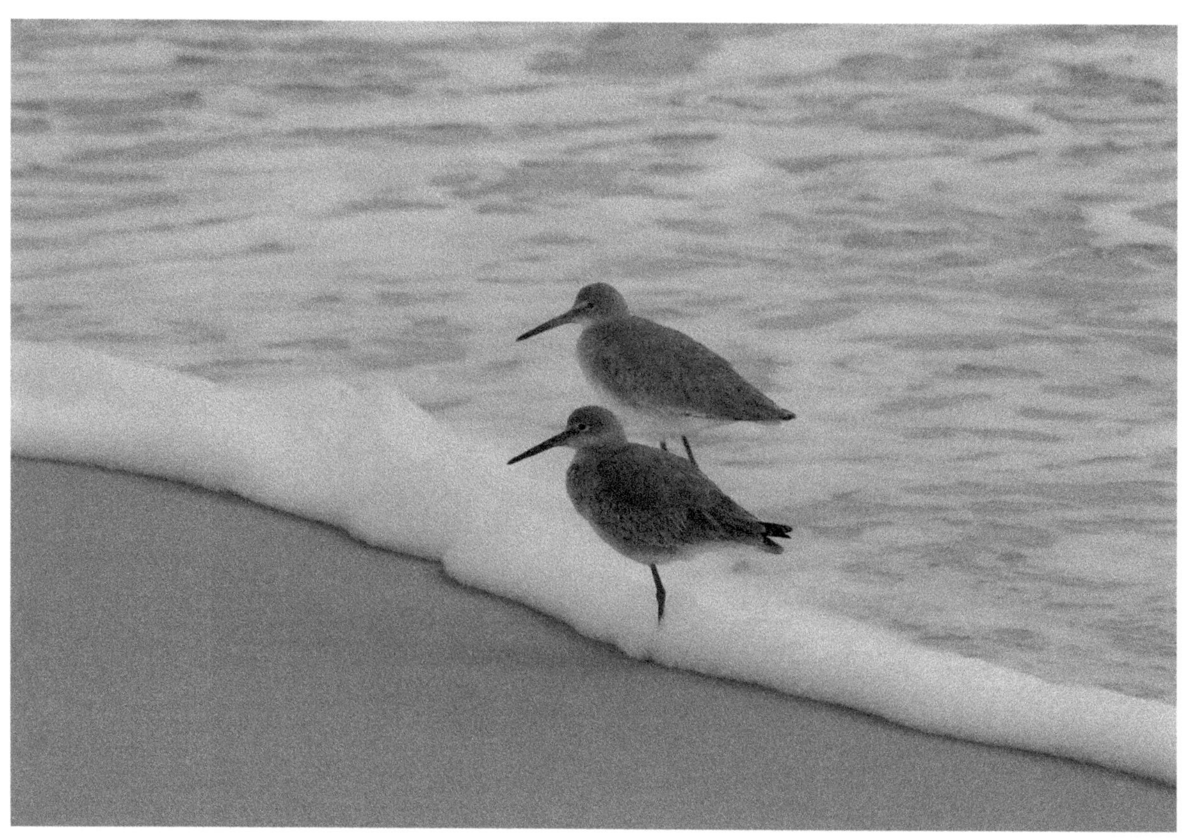

Willet

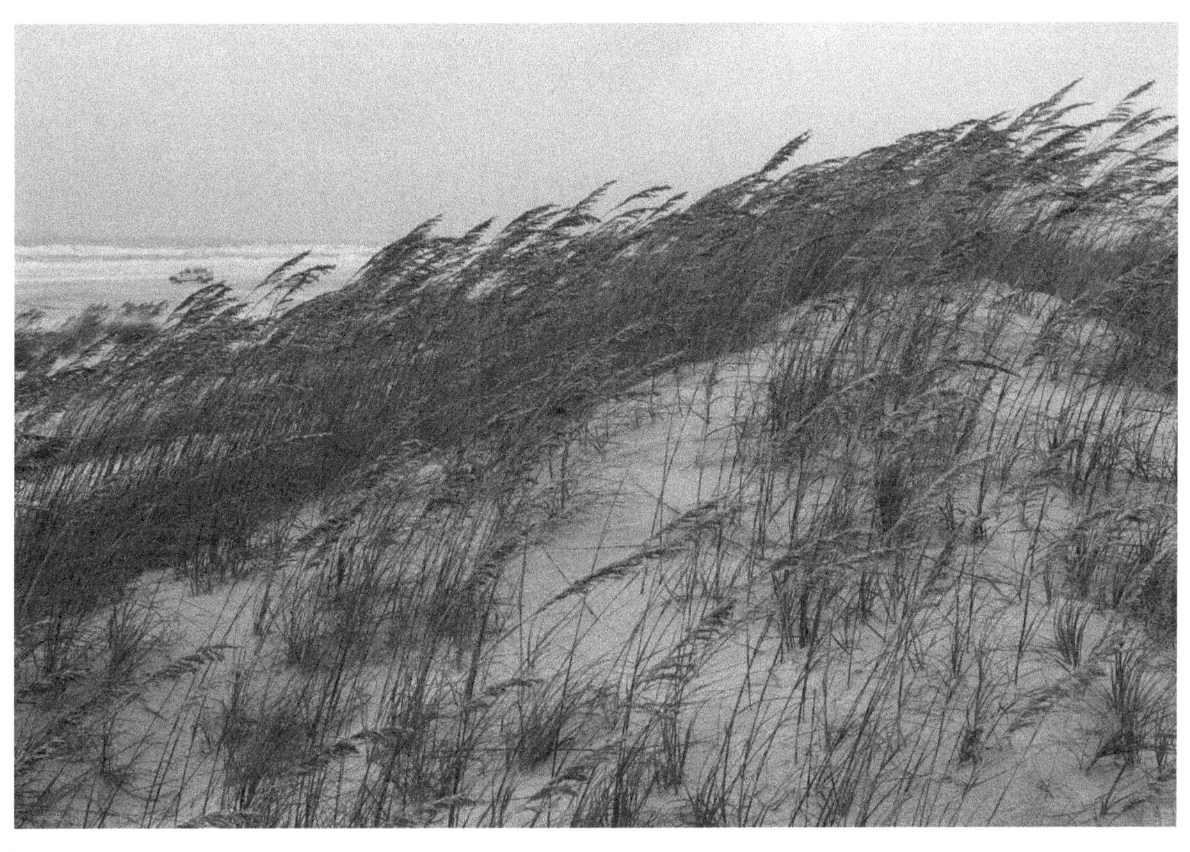

Little life guard truck

Fort Matanzas National Monument

As long ago as 1569, Spanish soldiers constructed a wooden watch tower somewhere near the southern end of Anastasia Island. This allowed sentries to look out over the Matanzas Inlet and search for sailing vessels gliding along the coastline.

Fort Matanzas was built between 1740 and 1742 on the west bank of the river overlooking the inlet. Some of the coquina was quarried from the vicinity of where today's Marineland is located. Additional coquina came from the quarries south of the watchtower on the northeast side of Anastasia Island. Cemented together with lime made from oyster shells burned down in kilns, the little fort was covered with a thick coat of white plaster. It would have made a bright landmark for those cruising off the coast.

The design of the fort is unique. A two story tower provided shelter for the sentries. A downspout located on the south wall carried water into a cistern from the upper observation deck. A fireplace on the ground floor provided warmth in the winter and a place to prepare daily meals. Cannon mounted on carriages and placed on wooden platforms on the gun deck could easily cover the mouth of the inlet a short distance away. They were never fired in defense of the fort.

When Florida became a United States territory after 1821, Fort Matanzas was viewed as a relic from the old Spanish days and was considered a site for tourists and fishermen. Mother nature slowly eroded the fort and the beach it was built upon.

In 1924, Fort Matanzas, Castillo de San Marcos and the Statue of Liberty were declared national monuments and became part of the National Park Service. Reconstruction of the little fort began shortly thereafter. In 1979 and 1980 the foundations were strengthened and a new gun-deck was poured.

Today one may visit the fort overlooking Rattlesnake Island and the beautiful salt water estuary of the Matanzas Inlet. A free ferry service operates from the visitor center to carry visitors across the river to the fort. Fort Matanzas National Monument anchors the southern end of Anastasia Island with over 350 acres of beach, majestic sand dunes and maritime forest. Commercial development will never be a problem at this important historic site. A nature trail, picnic areas, boardwalks over the sand dunes and plentiful fishing along the river and the beach make this a true jewel in the crown that is Anastasia Island.

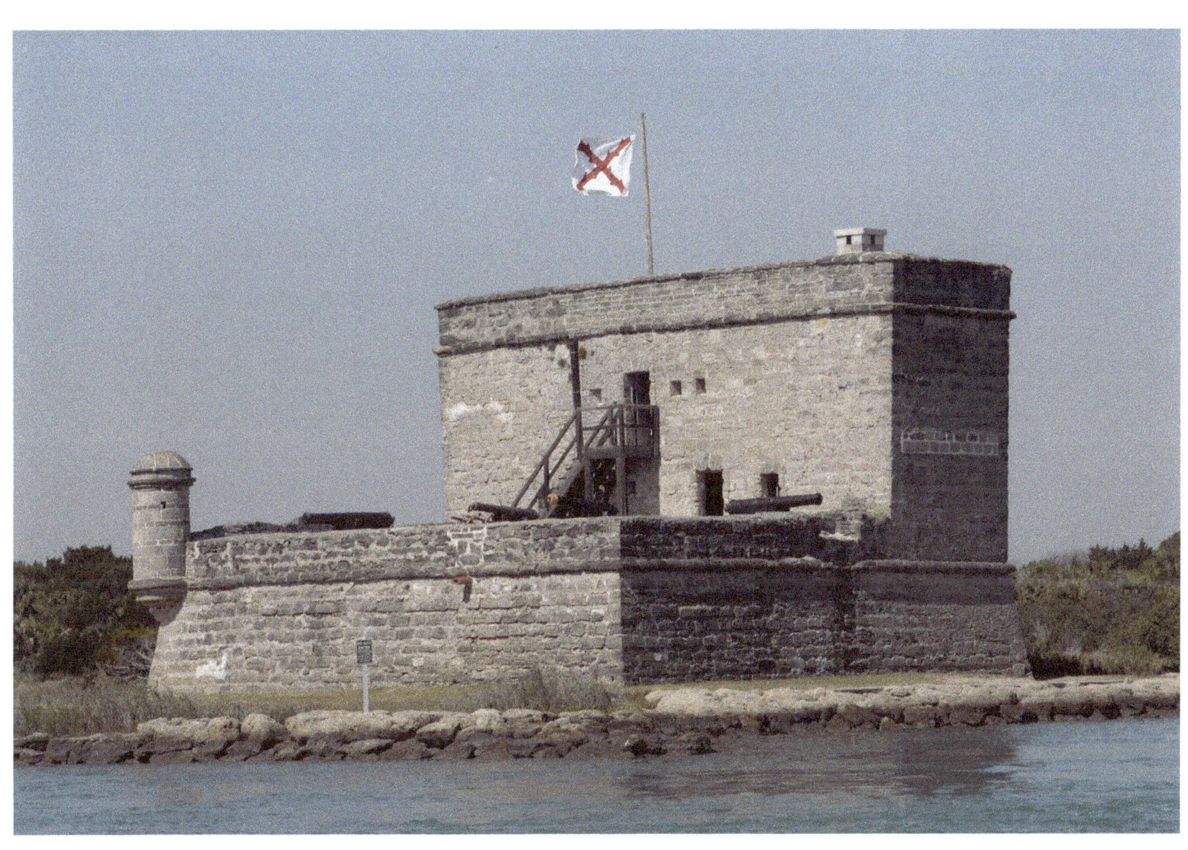

Fort Matanzas National Monument can be reached by boat.

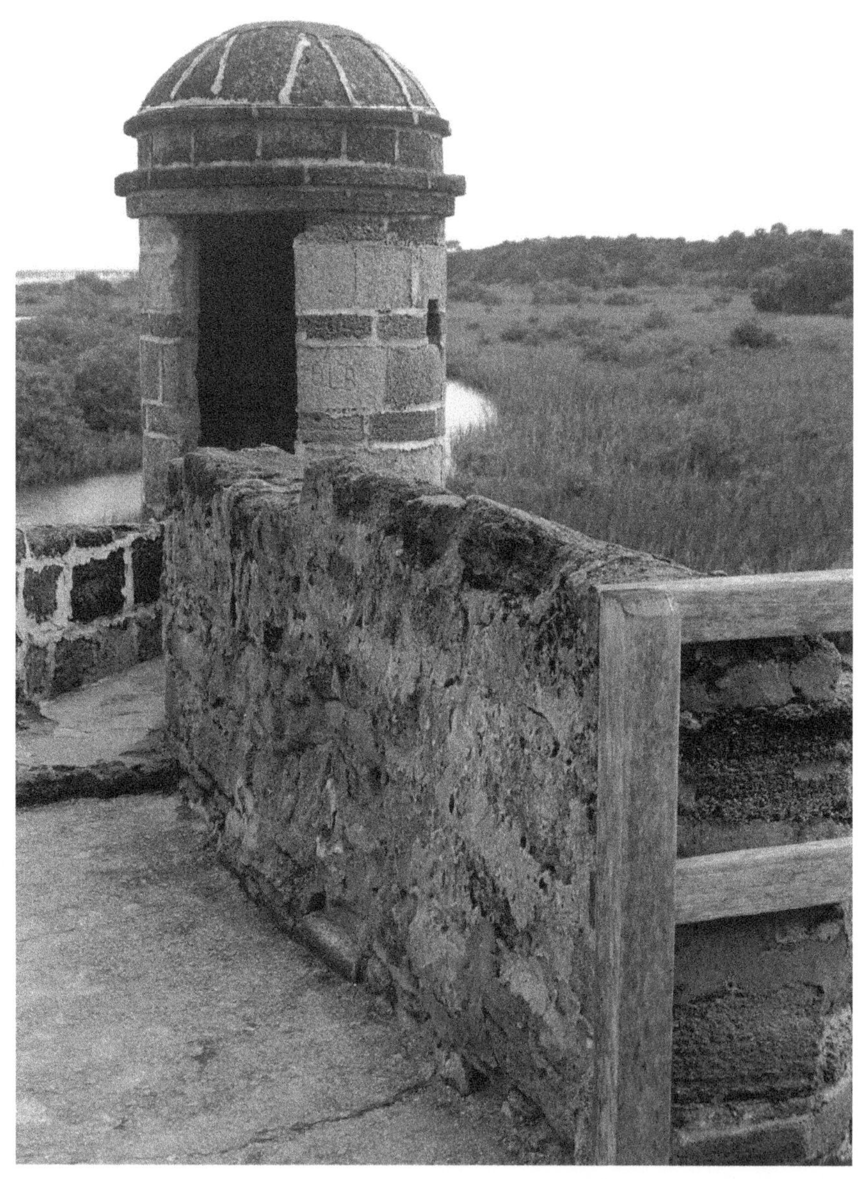

The reconstructed sentry box was finally finished in 1927.

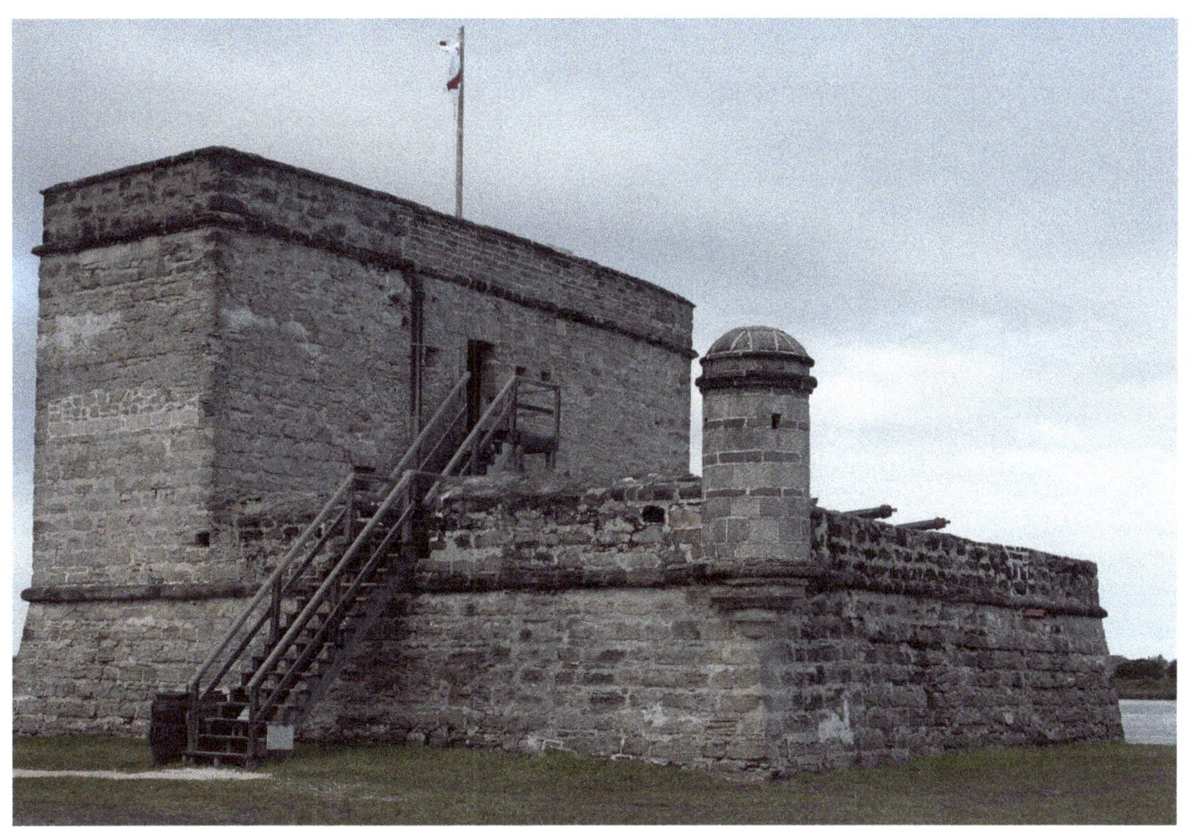

Fort Matanzas sits on Rattlesnake Island facing the Matanzas Inlet.

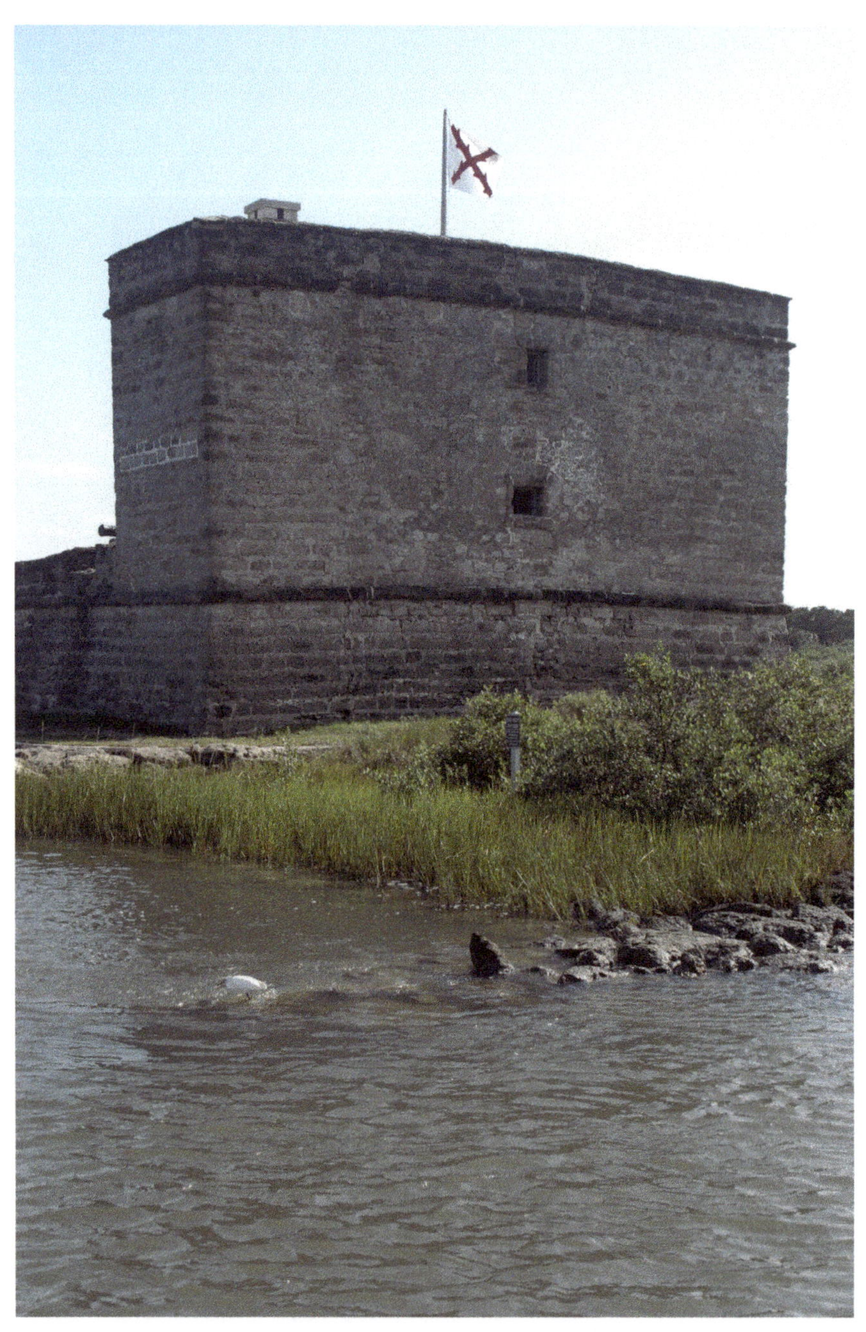

North façade of Fort Matanzas

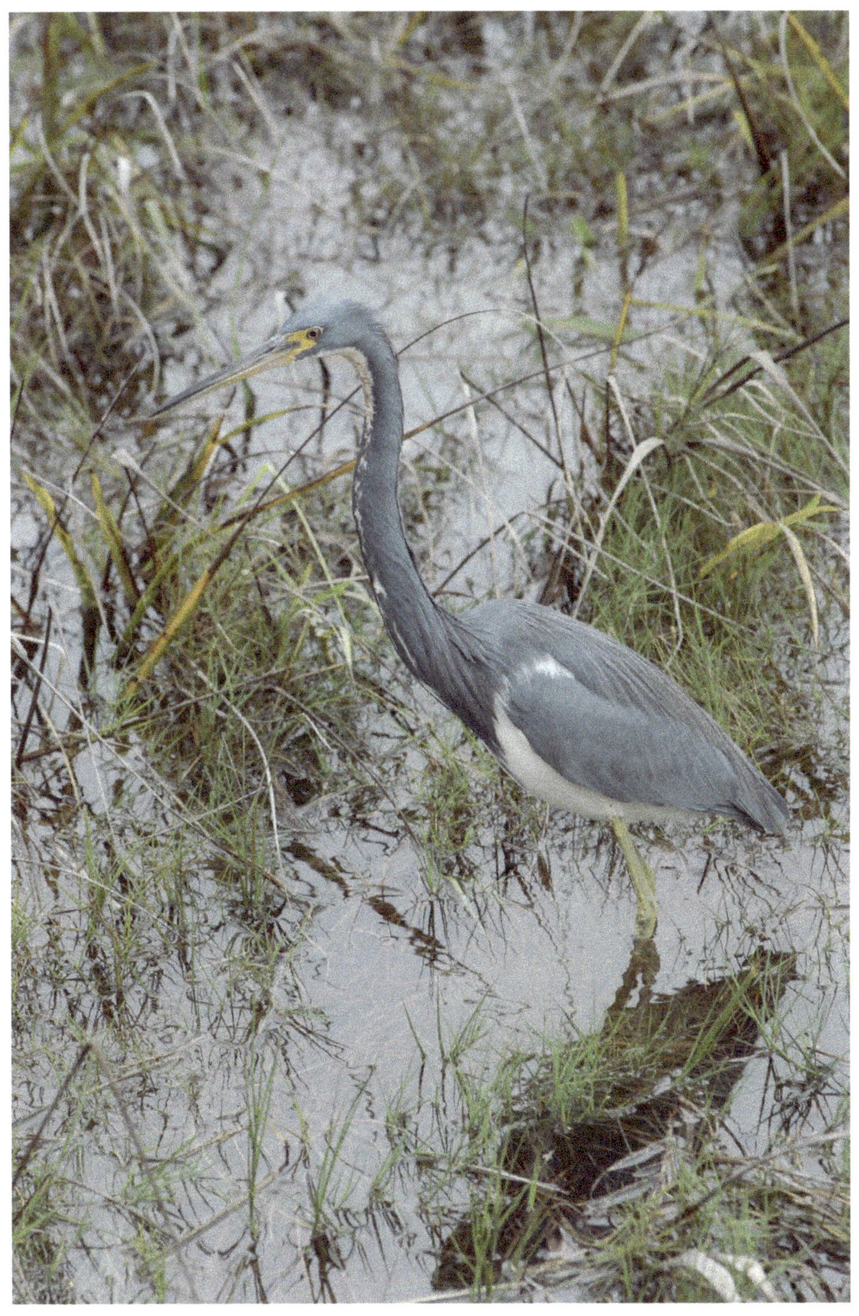

Louisiana Heron

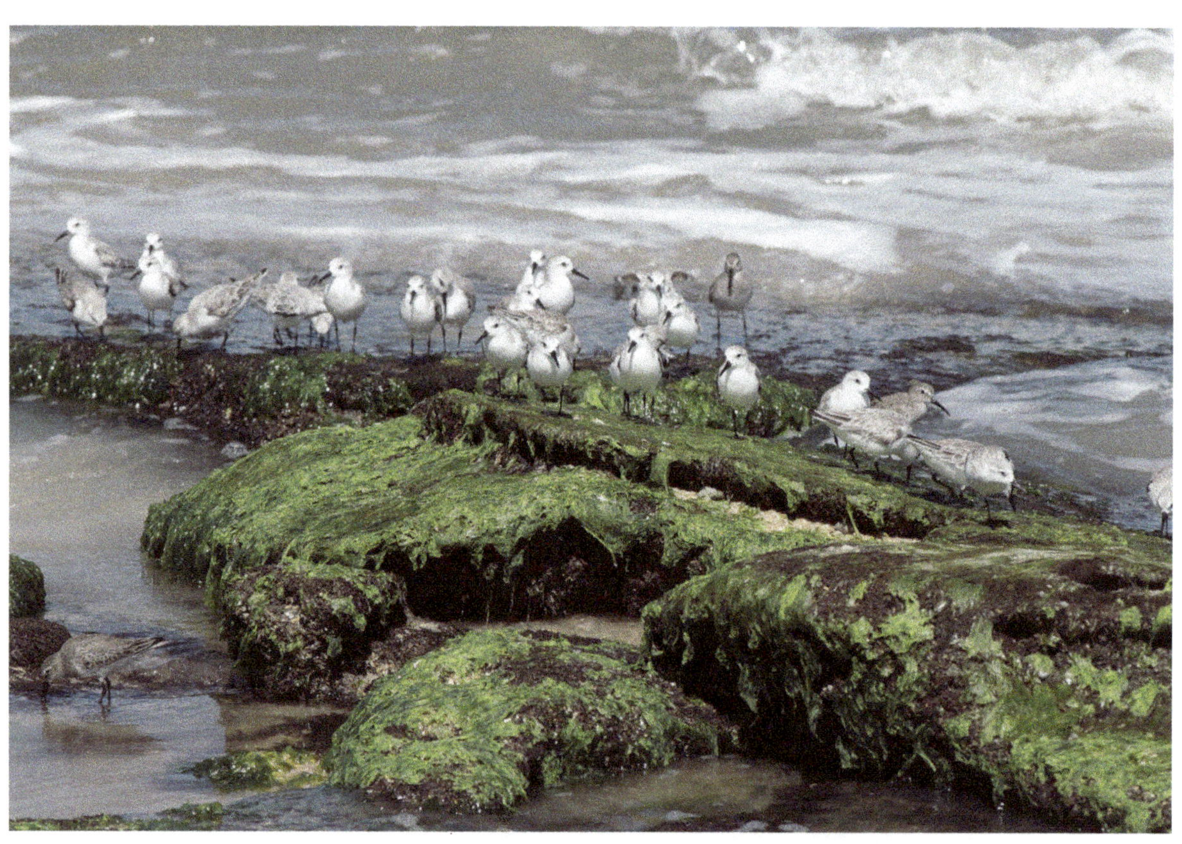

Sanderlings on a coquina outcropping.

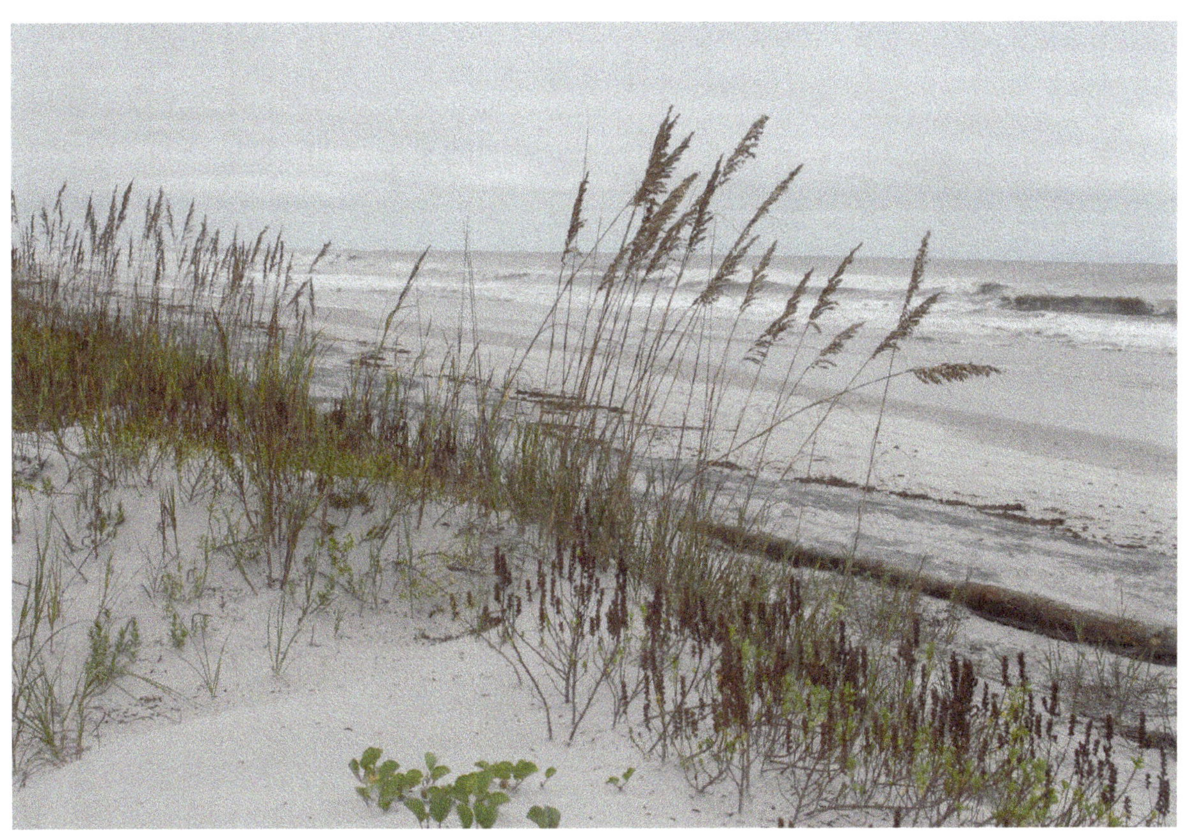

Overlooking the ever-changing coast.

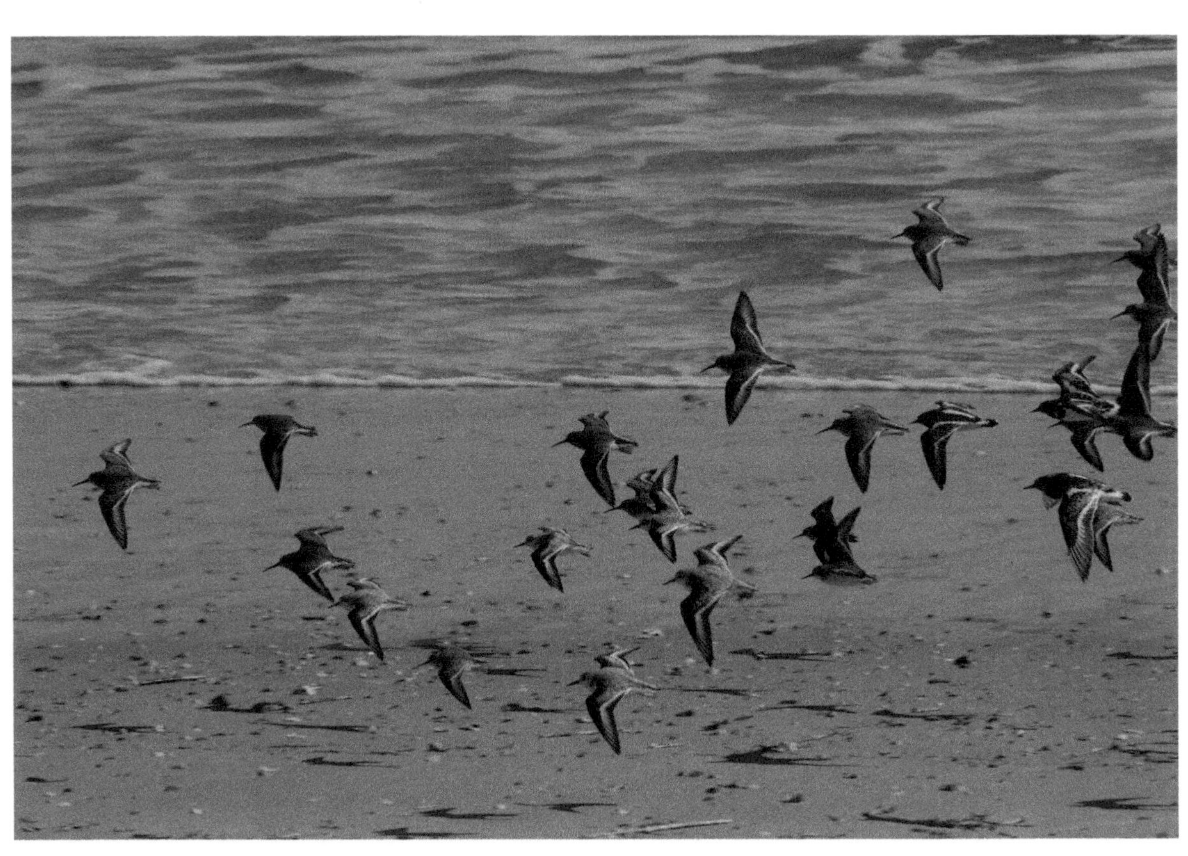

Sandpipers

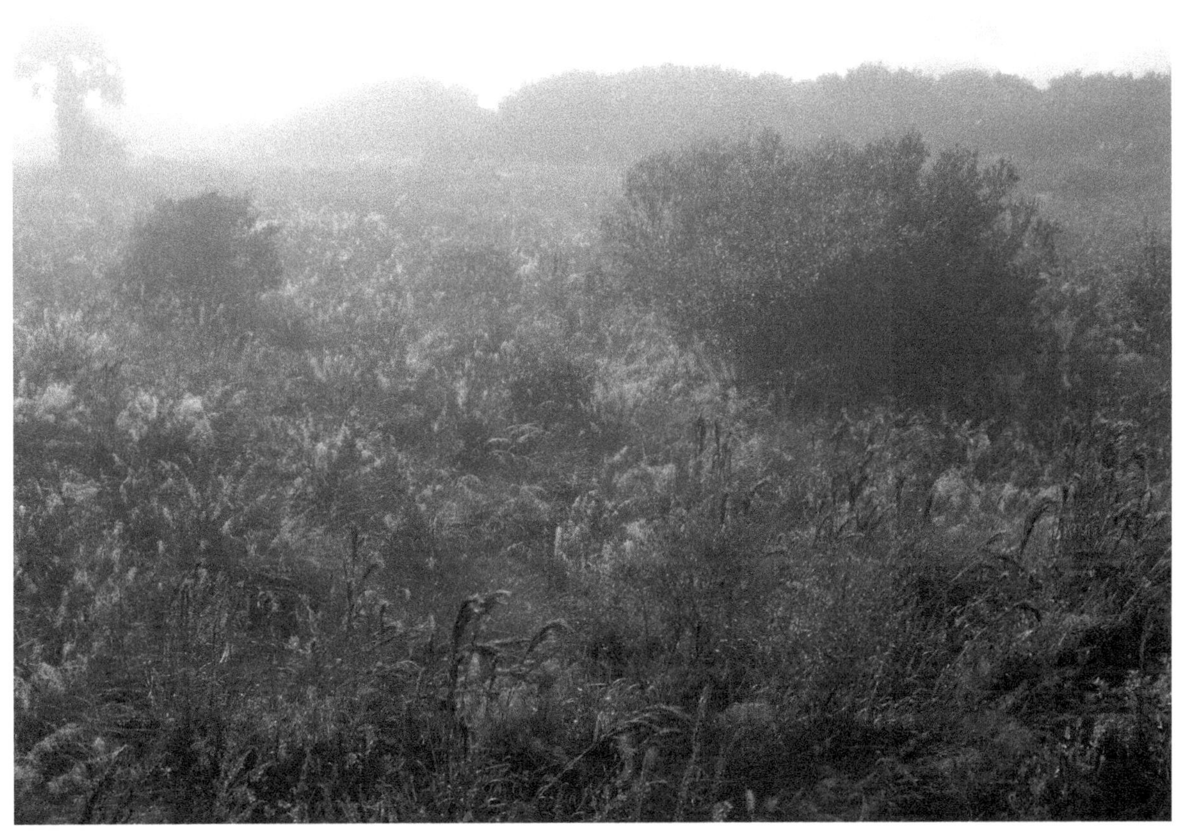

Winter sea fog.

Bibliography

Adams, William R., and Weaver III, Paul L. Historic Places of St. Augustine and St. Johns   County, A Visitor's Guide. Southern Heritage Press, 1993.

Adams, William R., and Shiver, Carl. The St. Augustine Alligator Farm, A Centennial History. Southern Heritage Press, 1993.

Anastasia State Park, A Brief History of Conch Island, 1996.

Arana, Luis Rafael. Notes on Fort Matanzas National Monument. St. Augustine Historical Society El Escribano, 1981.

Arana, Luis Rafael, and Manucy, Albert. The Building of Castillo de San Marcos. Eastern National Park and Monument Association, 1980.

Arnade, Charles W. The Architecture of Spanish St. Augustine, The Americas, October, 1961-Number 2.

Bowen, Beth Rogero, and the St. Augustine Historical Society. St. Augustine in the Gilded Age. Arcadia Publishing, 2008.

Bull, John, and Farrand, John, Jr. The Audubon Society Field Guide to North American Birds, Eastern Region. Alfred A. Knopf, New York, 1983.

Coote, Stephen. Drake The Life and Legend of an Elizabethan Hero. Simon and Schuster UK Ltd, 2003.

Edwards, Virginia. Stories of Old St. Augustine. C. F. Hamblen, Inc.,1973.

Hobbs, Robert. Earl Cunningham Painting, An American Eden. Harry N. Abrams, Inc., 1994.

Nolan, David. Fifty Feet in Paradise, The Booming of Florida. Harcourt Brace Jovanovich, 1984.

Nolan, David. The Houses of St. Augustine. Pineapple Press, Inc., 1995.

Parker, Susan. Griping and groaning is all part of the Oldest City's plan. St. Augustine Record, April 17, 2016.

Parker, Susan. First pier was a wonder of New Deal Era. St. Augustine Record, June 26, 2016.

Peterson, Roger Tory. A Field Guide To The Birds East Of The Rockies, Fourth Edition. Houghton Mifflin Company, Boston, 1980.

Raab, James W. Spain. Britain and The American Revolution in Florida, 1763-1783. McFarland & Company, Inc., Publishers, 2008.

Reynolds, Charles. The Standard Guide, St. Augustine. E. H. Reynolds, St. Augustine, Florida, 1892, 2004 Edition. Historic Print and Map Co., St. Augustine, Florida.

Secor, Don. Lighthouse Keeper's Log, St. Augustine Lighthouse, 1874-1948. St. Augustine Lighthouse, 1992.

Suddeth, Frank. Colonial St. Augustine's Nine Wooden Forts. Frank Suddeth, 1981.

Walch, Barbara. Frank B. Butler, Lincolnville Businessman and Founder of St. Augustine, Florida's Historic Black Beach. Rudolph B. Hadley, Sr., 1992.

Waterbury, Jean Parker. Editor: The Oldest City, St. Augustine Saga of Survival. The St. Augustine Historical Society, 1983.

Wright, J. Leitch. British St. Augustine. Historic St. Augustine Preservation Board, 1975.

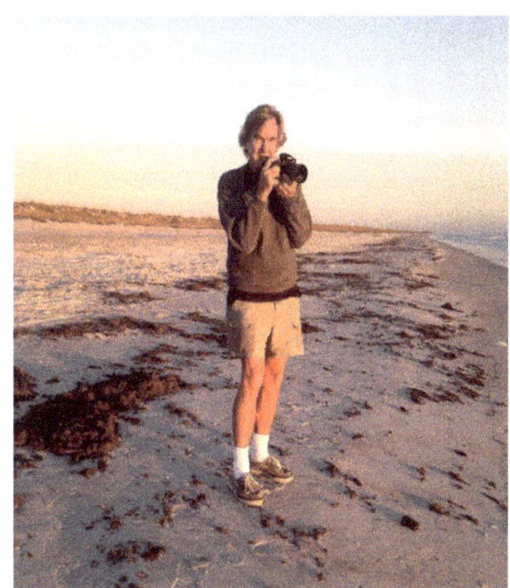

Photograph by Ellie Barrett

About the Author and Photographer

Kenneth Montier Barrett, Jr., grew up prowling the sand dunes and tide lines of Anastasia Island. After earning a degree in Journalism from the University of Florida he joined the National Park Service, firing the cannons at the Castillo, leading nature walks at Fort Matanzas and curating the photography collection.

A Transatlantic sailor and ship's cook aboard George Dryden's Schooner, Lita, he joined the faculty of the Art Department at Flagler College, beginning a long love affair with teaching.

An exhibitor in Florida Art Shows since 1972, his work has been used in numerous publications. The St. Augustine Historical Society has published many of his original photographs. The Houses of St. Augustine published by Pineapple Press is in it's third printing. Florida's Colonial Architectural Heritage, Heart and Soul of Florida and Walking St. Augustine published by the University Press of Florida all display his viewpoint.

Archives of the Department of the Interior, Florida State Archives, The National Park Service, the St. Augustine Lighthouse Museum and St. Augustine Historical Society to name a few, all house his photographs.

A beachcomber by vocation and avocation he continues to photograph the ever-changing Florida shoreline.

Contact

Facebook.com/Florida-Heritage-Photography